Born in Augsburg, Germany, in 1898, Bertolt Brecht did medical duty in World War I and after the war began writing the ballads, poetry, and plays that brought him success in German theatre by the time he was 24. The next years saw Marxism and Communism as political forces which influenced his *The Three-Penny Opera*, *A Man's a Man*, and *The Measures Taken*. With Hitler's ascent, Brecht went into exile and his fame and financial success suddenly ended—his chances for writing and producing new works were reduced and the possibilities of getting new plays produced in German were diminished. In 1936 he became co-editor of the anti-Fascist *Das Wort*, but in 1941 was forced to flee to the United States where he secured a living with Hollywood work. Returning to Berlin in 1948, he was received as the grand old man of theatre and was master of The Berliner Ensemble until his death in 1956.

Crosscurrents/MODERN CRITIQUES

Harry T. Moore, *General Editor*

BERTOLT BRECHT
The Despair and the Polemic

Charles R. Lyons

WITH A PREFACE BY

Harry T. Moore

Carbondale and Edwardsville

SOUTHERN ILLINOIS UNIVERSITY PRESS

FEFFER & SIMONS, INC.

London and Amsterdam

For Leila

Preface

Bertolt Brecht has become one of the few twentieth-century dramatists whom critics and public alike agree is of the first rank. He is something of an anomaly in that he is a Communist author highly regarded in capitalist countries. Yet Brecht's communism probably didn't go too deep, for, after the Second World War, when he was given his own theater in East Berlin, he was unable to manufacture red-starred propagandist plays.

He had begun writing while serving as a medical orderly in the earlier world war. There was, for example, his satiric "Legende vom toten Soldaten" ("Legend of the Dead Soldier"). Brecht used to sing this in cafés, accompanying himself on a guitar, when he was a medical student after the war. It is a ballad about the dead soldier revived by the conscription-board doctors because the Kaiser needs more troopers. The "Legend" amused the café crowds except for the militarists among them.

Leaving his medical studies, the young Brecht soon became a playwright. Eventually he left Germany (although not a Jew) and sought refuge in various countries; he was for a while a Hollywood screenwriter. After the Second World War he took out and retained Austrian citizenship, though he spent most of his time in East Germany. He died at fifty-seven, of coronary thrombosis.

In the present book, Charles R. Lyons deals with what he considers Brecht's major plays, beginning with Baal. That was the first play Brecht wrote, but it was the second

to be produced. As Mr. Lyons points out, Baal was composed at white heat in four days—in Munich, 1918. It
was written partly out of irritation, as Mr. Lyons also
indicates, with a play of Hanns Johst. Baal was first performed in Liepzig in 1923; in 1926, the first Berlin production featured Oskar Homolka.

Brecht's first play to be produced, however, was the
second one which he wrote: Trommeln in der Nacht
(Drums in the Night). Mr. Lyons doesn't deal with this,
and he is probably right in thinking of it as minor, but
it is interesting to note as Brecht's first large-scale encounter with the public. It is a play with the returned-
soldier theme, and when it was printed in 1922 the text
contained "Legend of the Dead Soldier." The play was
performed in Munich and Berlin in that year, and for the
opening at Munich the influential drama critic Herbert
Ihering came down from Berlin and later wrote that a
twenty-four-year-old poet had "changed the literary countenance of Germany overnight." Brecht won the Kleist
prize that year as the outstanding German dramatist.

Now we have Brecht launched upon his career, which
included theater directorships as well as the continued
writing of poetry. It is useful to know these matters before turning to Mr. Lyons's study of the major plays.

It is a thorough study, far more so than we are used
to in the case of Brecht. It covers seven of the dramas,
from Baal to Der kaukasische Kreidekreis (The Caucasian
Chalk Circle). The author is concerned with the integrity
of Brecht's vision, which remained essentially the same
through all his various expressions of it. The usual tendency is to show a pre-Marxian and a Marxian Brecht, but
Mr. Lyons doesn't find this double man in Brecht's writing.

Mr. Lyons's work is rich in insights, and it convincingly
makes its way through various arguments and expositions
as it considers the work of this man who was, as his
biographer Martin Esslin points out, unable to meet the
requests of Party leaders that he write something in aid

of their cause. Mr. Lyons's book helps to suggest that Brecht couldn't do this because he was too deeply committed to individualism.

HARRY T. MOORE

Southern Illinois University
April 23, 1968

Acknowledgments

I wish to thank the following editors for permission to use material from *Baal, The Measures Taken, In the Jungle of the Cities, A Man's a Man, Mother Courage, Galileo, The Caucasian Chalk Circle,* and *Tales from the Calender,* by Bertolt Brecht (copyright © 1949, 1953, and 1955 by Suhrkamp Verlag, Berlin und Frankfurt am Main); from *Seven Plays by Bertolt Brecht,* Eric Bentley, ed. (copyright © 1961 by Eric Bentley), reprinted by permission of Mr. Bentley and Grove Press, New York, N. Y.; from *The Theatre of Bertolt Brecht,* by John Willett, copyright © 1959, 1960 by John Willett, reprinted by permission of New Directions Publishing Corporation—all rights reserved; from *Seven Types of Ambiguity,* by William Empson, reprinted by permission of New Directions Publishing Corporation—all rights reserved; from *Psychoanalytic Explorations in Art* by Ernst Kris, reprinted by permission of International Universities Press, Inc., New York, N. Y.; from *On The Limits of Poetry* by Allen Tate, reprinted by permission of Mr. Tate and Alan Swallow, Denver, who published *Collected Essays* by Allen Tate in 1959; from Introduction to *Brecht: A Collection of Critical Essays,* by Peter Demetz, © 1962, reprinted by permission of Prentice-Hall, Inc., Englewood Cliffs, N. J.; from *Brecht on Theatre* translated by John Willett, reprinted by permission of Hill and Wang, Inc.; from *Anatomy of Criticism,* by Northrop Frye, © 1957, reprinted by permission of Princeton University Press; from *Being and Nothingness* by Jean-Paul Sartre, trans. by Hazel E. Barnes, reprinted by permission of Philosophical Library; from *Principles of Literary Criticism* by I. A. Richards, reprinted by permission of Harcourt, Brace & World, Inc.; from *The Theatre of Bertolt Brecht,* by John Willett, reprinted by permission of Methuen & Co., Ltd.; from *Brecht* on Theatre, by Bertolt Brecht, trans. John Willett, reprinted by permission of Methuen & Co., Ltd.; from The Life of Galileo by Bertolt Brecht, trans. Desmond Vesey, reprinted by permission of Methuen & Co. Ltd.; from Tales from the Calender, by Bertolt Brecht, prose trans. Yvonne Kapp, poetry trans. Michael Hamburger, reprinted by permission of Methuen & Co., Ltd.; from the Preface to An Anthology of German Expressionist Drama—a Prelude to the Absurd, Walter H. Sokel, editor, © 1963 by Walter H. Sokel, reprinted by permission of Doubleday, Inc.; from Brecht, The Man and His Work, by Martin Esslin, © 1959 by Martin Esslin, reprinted by permission of Doubleday, Inc.; from Hofmannsthal's "Prologue to Brecht's Baal," trans. by Alfred Schwarz—first published Tulane Drama Review, Vol. 6, No. 1 (T13, Autumn, 1961), copyright 1961, Tulane Drama Review, reprinted by permission of the publishers; from "Brecht's Galileo," by Gunter Rohrmoser, trans. J. F. Sammons, Brecht: A Collection of Critical Essays, ed. Peter Demetz, reprinted by permission of August Bagel Verlag, Dusseldorf; from "Mother Courage and her Children," by Franz Norbert Mennemeier, trans. J. F. Sammons, in Brecht: A Collection of Critical Essays, Peter Demetz, ed., reprinted by permission of August Bagel Verlag, Dusseldorf; from Bertolt Brecht by Ronald Gray, reprinted by permission of Oliver & Boyd Ltd., Edinburgh; from Selected Poems of Bertolt Brecht, trans. by H. R. Hays, copyright, 1947, by Bertolt Brecht and H. R. Hays, reprinted by permission of Harcourt, Brace & World, Inc.

C. R. L.

Contents

Introduction

In the past several years there has been a great deal written and published in English about the work of Bertolt Brecht. Eric Bentley's translations, especially the collection *Seven Plays of Bertolt Brecht*,[1] Martin Esslin's critical biography, *Brecht: The Man and his Work*,[2] and John Willett's *The Theatre of Bertolt Brecht*,[3] have accomplished the significant work of making Brecht known to the English-speaking world. The perceptive criticism which these men have given us has provided a foundation upon which all further study of Brecht must be built.

Bentley's vital and sensitive translations have proved invaluable in the development of an understanding and appreciative American audience for the special riches of Brecht's plays—in the theater and in individual study. The tasks which Esslin and Willett have undertaken in their broad and inclusive studies of the playwright were difficult and significantly successful. In Esslin's work, especially, there is a thorough job of relating Brecht's plays to his biography and to the specific philosophical, sociological, and historical moments for which it was written. Esslin's critical analyses are keenly perceptive. However, the larger task of his book precludes detailed interpretations of the plays. It seems to me that at this point in the critical study of Brecht, there needs to be extensive discussion of the plays themselves, close readings of the texts which will work to illuminate the profound complexity of Brecht's apprehension of human experience.

This study examines a sequence of Brecht's major plays, ranging from his earliest dramatic composition, *Baal*, to his last significant play, *The Caucasian Chalk Circle*. While this discussion of the nature of Brecht's plays attempts to provide full interpretative analyses of the major plays, its special aim is to examine them in terms of their integrity. Brecht's primary concern is the nature of human action, the limits of which are imposed upon the human will as it attempts to assert itself. From one perspective, it is possible to divide Brecht's work into two major periods, the pre-Marxist and the Marxist. It is undeniable that Brecht's early plays are those of anguish in which Brecht insists upon the hopelessness of the human condition. Correspondingly, there is an explicit assumption in the Marxist plays that there is a possibility of changing the world. However, the external polemic in these plays cannot disguise a continuing despair, and throughout Brecht's poetry and drama there is a persistent cry for compassion as the playwright responds to human suffering. In the introduction to his edition of *Seven Plays*, Eric Bentley criticizes the tendency to think in terms of "two Brechts," and he makes the following judgment concerning the integrity of Brecht's creative work:

> It would be strange indeed if a poet could cut his creative life so neatly in half. I believe that one can only get the impression that Brecht did so if one is blinded by political prejudice. If Brecht had a divided nature, it was—as the word *nature* implies—divided all his life long. Such a division is discernible in every major play. Otherwise, the lifework of Brecht has a most impressive unity: what is found in the late plays is found in the early ones, and *vice versa*. This is not to say that there is no development, nor is it to deny that Brecht *attempted* something like the total change which the doctrinaires on both sides attribute to him. One might say he providentially failed in this attempt. More probably, he surely if dimly knew what he was doing. Behind the attempt to change was the knowledge that one cannot—and a wily, conniving refusal to go to all lengths in attempting the impossible. This is speculation about the

fact of unity in Brecht's work. About the fact itself there can be little doubt.

Necessary to the appreciation of this fact is the discovery or rediscovery of the early plays, particularly *Baal* and *In the Swamp* [*In the Jungle of the Cities*]." [4]

The unity of Brecht's work, in my opinion, is directed by the fact that his plays are, in a sense, explorations of the quality of a single human action—the futile attempt of the human will to assert itself in a free act. This attempt, in other words, is a struggle to attain a sense of consistent and meaningful identity, to separate the unique and personal aspect of being from its environment. *Baal*, for example, is an ambiguous affirmation of its hero's vitality, but, on the other hand, it is a nihilistic declaration that even a vital creature such as Baal is, in reality, the passive victim of instinct. In *Baal*, Brecht does not actually oppose will and instinct, but there is an implicit judgment that Baal's destructive energy is a kind of evil. In the more complex early play, *In the Jungle of the Cities*, Brecht explores the isolation of the human soul. In this play, the will attempts to assert itself in its endeavor to achieve contact with another human being. However, in a world in which human relationship only exists in sexual use, the will accepts the futility of such an assertion.

In these early plays, human instinct is seen as a destructive energy to which man is the passive victim; and yet, paradoxically, the characters of these plays seem to realize their identity most fully as they surrender to the instinctive desires which dominate them. It is important to realize that Brecht conceived this surrender to instinct, however, as a consumption, a devouring. These plays are pervaded with what Lüthy describes as a "rhetoric of decomposition;" and Esslin states: "The process of nature is seen as one of incessant birth and decay, with human consciousness powerless to break the eternal cycle." [5]

As I mentioned above, one aspect of Brecht's dramatizations of the will is an exploration of the nature of human identity. In the Marxist plays, the individual will is sacrificed to the collective, and in A *Man's a Man,* a comedy which provides a prelude to these plays, Brecht describes the process of transforming a man's identity. Yet this is an equivocal work, and while Brecht later attempted to use it as a demonstration that human beings could be reconstructed in better images, the inhumanity of the concept that function should determine identity is decried in the play.

In the didactic plays, which are Brecht's earliest and most specifically Marxist works, Brecht clearly opposes reason and instinct. In these versions of the typical Brechtian drama, the will's attempt to act independently is destructive. As the discussion of *The Measures Taken* will clarify, Brecht, apparently unconsciously, invests the agency of rational control, The Party, with the same devouring qualities which are held by Nature in the early plays. The Young Comrade suffers the energies of his own instincts and asserts his will to control them. However, that assertion is, actually, a surrender to the will of The Party and the acceptance of his own death. While the intent of this play is an affirmation of the value of The Party, it describes the terrible pain incurred when the unique identity of a human being is sacrificed to function. Esslin declares

> after he [Brecht] had surrendered himself to what he regarded as a supremely rational creed, he depicted the rational side of his characters as an element of villainy in them—though one that was necessary for their survival in society. He, of course, always argued that after the victory of Communism this conflict between reason and instinct would disappear. But the fact remains that a practical approach to the problem of survival and success—such as the highly realistic tactics of Communism demanded—is consistently shown in a negative light in Brecht's later work.[6]

The tension in Brecht's poetry is not only a conflict between the passive acceptance of emotional energy and the rational control of the will; it is also a tension between a sense that man is a passive victim who suffers forces which are external to his own consciousness and a sense that, in the assertion of his will, man can determine action. Although it seems not to be a conscious exploration, Brecht's mature plays deal with the essential question of human action—the possibility of a pure assertion. In his explicitly written statements concerning the ambiguous response to *Mother Courage,* Brecht assumed that Courage had the possibility of choice, the opportunity to assert herself in opposition to the logic of exploitation and the business of war: "the play always left the equally petty-bourgeois Courage quite free to choose whether or no she should take part [in the war]." [7] And yet, within the world projected in *Mother Courage,* is Courage free to assert herself? In this world, the war, "the sum of everybody's business operations," is the sociological context—the human condition. Anna Fierling's commitment to her business is a realistic acceptance of a logic which governs the world. It is a logic of the exploitation and consumption of the other. In one sense, Courage's submission to this logic is a rational judgment, the use of a reason which denies and controls her feelings. *Mother Courage* is the tragic answer to the negation of identity in *A Man's a Man.* In the acceptance of her identity as business woman, she denies and then loses her identity as mother until all she has left is her business function. In the conflict between reason and instinct in *Mother Courage,* Anna Fierling's reason allows her to survive. Kattrin, her daughter, is the victim of her own instinctive compassion; and, while her action is suicidal, Brecht clearly sees it as the primary value of the play. The consequence of Kattrin's act of warning the citizens of Halle, saving them from massacre, is her death; and yet, Kattrin has realized the satisfaction of her will in a determined action. Even though this action is also seen as a surrender to instinct, it has more the quality of a willed action than Anna Fierling's rational submission to the logic of exploitation.

The relentless exploration of guilt in *Galileo* is equally ambiguous. The obvious ethical structure of this play focuses the blame for the atomic explosion in Hiroshima, the misuse of modern science in the destruction of man by man, upon Galileo's recantation. Yet Galileo, like Mother Courage, is unable to make the choice which will deny his own life while it affirms the value of human existence. Compounding the ambiguity, Brecht makes Galileo's appetite for life's pleasures the source of his scientific discoveries. His surrender to instinct is the very source of his reason; consequently, that reason must serve and not deny his physical comfort. His will is subject to the energies of his own instinct, and, like Baal and every other Brechtian hero, his attempt to make a free assertion is futile.

In discussing *The Caucasian Chalk Circle* in terms of the central Brechtian drama, it is important to see that the instinctive movement of the compassionate act is defined in this play as something dangerous to the self, "terrible," but as a strong value. Grusha, like Kattrin, suffers an instinctive compassion, and her action is irrational, unwise. But in this romantic dream of a play, Grusha is not made to suffer the ultimate consequences of her compassion. In a typical romantic structure, she suffers for a time, in an intense but short-lived agony or ordeal, but, eventually, she is freed from that suffering and given the gift of an infinite happiness with son and lover. However, it is important to realize that Brecht accomplishes this celebration of compassion within the framework of a fiction. *The Caucasian Chalk Circle* is not the graphic, realistic projection of human behavior that *Mother Courage* is. Implicit in the epic structure of Brecht's version of the Grimmelshausen heroine is a stark awareness that in the real world such "courage," such greed, such exploitation exist. That consciousness of a real and cruel world exists in *The Caucasian Chalk Circle*; but, in this play, the poet seems to share with the audience an enjoyment of the aesthetic illusion that compassion can exist, freely and creatively, in a sordid, suffering world and be rewarded with happiness rather than self-destruction.

This study of Brecht's most significant plays discusses them in terms of their integrity, the unity of their concern, and—in this perspective—it is possible to see both the content and the form of Brechtian drama in its development from the disorganized chaos of *Baal's* satire of Expressionism to the sophisticated imitation of primitive romance in *The Caucasian Chalk Circle*.

This study does not ignore form in its thematic concern. Brechtian form is infinitely related to its content. Brecht's own aesthetic theories are discussed at those points at which they are needed to clarify discussions of structure. While there is no extensive analysis of Brecht's concepts of "Epic Theatre" (since that kind of exposition is available elsewhere), I have referred to Brecht's own critical writing, most specifically, in discussing the relationship between play and audience which Brecht assumed. Peter Demetz makes the following comment:

> Brecht's theory does not necessarily add to our understanding or to our undisturbed evaluation of his plays. Although it would be misleading to say that the changing system of his ideas and the theatrical universe of his plays are far apart—for they converge in the Thirties—their relationship is, at best, a loose, intermittent and paradoxical one. As no other modern playwright, Brecht was constantly on the alert to prevent his audience from enjoying his plays incorrectly, but again and again the creations of the playwright defeated the efforts of the theorist; again and again the play itself assumed a radiant autonomy that calmly disdained any belated attempt to make it a servant to ideology or intent.[8]

Brecht's aesthetic theories, which were continuously being refined, began their course in the antirealistic movement of German Expressionism and insistently demanded that the experience within the theatre should be obviously artificial so that the spectator's imagination would focus upon the social reality which was being discussed in the dramatic action. Brecht's theatricalism is certainly an aspect of the larger antirealistic movement which includes such diverse playwrights as Pirandello and, more recently, Beckett. However, Brecht's effort to disintegrate the sense of illusion in the dramatic event derives from a conception of reality radically different from the more typical manifestations of antirealism. For example, Pirandello's theatricalism invests as much reality in the artifice of the performance as in the subject itself. In the complex fragmentation of reality in the Pirandello play, the sense of a comprehensible and integral reality does not obtain. In Beckett's drama, the focus is upon the individual consciousness, and Beckett's explorations of phenomena all take place within this center. In the disintegration of realism which has taken place in modern drama, objective reality has been replaced by a reality determined by the subjective consciousness. Explicitly, of course, Brecht's drama assumes an objective reality as the field for consideration. However, that drama does move into subjectivity as it concerns the drama of the will in its futile attempt to assert itself. This intense concern with the individual is, certainly, one of the factors which allow Demetz to claim that Brecht's plays are in paradoxical relationship to his theories. It is impossible, I admit, to see this relationship as anything but paradoxical. Yet Brecht's response to the individual will repeatedly focused upon the effort the human consciousness was exerting in order to commune with another human being. His despair prevails, we know, because in the plays that effort remains futile—until the obvious fiction of *The Caucasian Chalk Circle*. However, it must be remembered that the ideal of the harmonious collective was, for Brecht, a state of being in which the individual will would be free to act according to its own resources and desires and exist in creative relation to others. Implicit in the comprehension of the whole is the comprehension of the single man.

Earlier versions of chapters 1, 2, and 6 appeared in *Modern Drama*, *Drama Survey*, and *The Germanic Review* respectively. I am grateful to the editors of these magazines for permission to use that material.

I would like to use this occasion to mark a special debt.

It would be impossible to measure the inspiration, influence, keen criticism, ideas, and encouragement given me by Professor James Kerans, an exceptional teacher and a very good friend. I am also very indebted to Professor Robert Loper of Stanford University for his criticism and good advice and Dean William W. Melnitz of the University of California, Los Angeles, for his thoughtful advice and consistent encouragement. I would also like to express my appreciation to Martin Esslin who read the early papers on Brecht and first suggested that they were the beginning of a book. Two other colleagues, Professors Herbert Lindenberger and David Bronsen of Washington University, have been very helpful in reading the manuscript and offering suggestions for its improvement.

CHARLES R. LYONS

23 October 1967
Elsah, Illinois

Bertolt Brecht

Baal: The Celebration of Destructive Nature

Baal, Bertolt Brecht's first play, is an uncontrolled adoles-
cent outburst. The first draft of this unrestrained and
chaotic work was produced in four days in 1918 while
Brecht was a medical student in Munich. Martin Esslin,
Brecht's fine biographer, describes Brecht's acute irritation
at *Der Einsame*, Hanns Johst's idealized celebration of
Christian Dietrich Grabbe, the dissolute German poet;
and Esslin repeats the story that *Baal* was written because
a friend challenged Brecht to write a better play than
Johst's drama.[1] The Grabbe figure in *Der Einsame* assumes the expressionist's image of the poet as a special,
unique being who should not be subject to the restrictions
of bourgeois society. Brecht's presentation of the dissolute
poet in the character of Baal does ridicule Johst's idealization of Grabbe, and, on one level, Brecht's first play is a
satire of the expressionist's amoral conception of the poet.

Brecht's hero is a being free from any moral commitment, and he ranges through heterosexual and homosexual adventures in an erotic fantasy, using people and
discarding them along the way. The comic exaggeration
certainly derives from Brecht's satiric intent to ridicule
Johst's play. However, Baal is an extremely complex work.
Brecht, of course, was unused to handling dramatic conventions and inexperienced in restraining his own intuition
and controlling his creative energy. *Baal* reads as if all the
young poet's emotional and intellectual energies demanded a voice. The play echoes Brecht's disgust at
Johst's sentimentality, rehearses the homosexual relation-

ship of Rimbaud and Verlaine, echoing Rimbaud's own poetic images,[2] and consciously attempts to be an affront to the spectator's sensibilities. In a series of apparently disjointed episodes, Brecht tells the story of Baal, the poet-singer. The play begins with a comic episode in which Baal attempts to seduce the wife of a man who is considering publishing his poems. The bestial Baal is blind to all concerns other than the purest enjoyment of sensuality. He listens to his friend's erotic description of his fiancée, and then seduces the innocent girl himself, driving her to suicide in the river. After another affair with a girl named Sophie, whom he impregnates, Baal embarks on a series of homosexual adventures with his friend, Ekart, punctuating this erotic male relationship with frequent sexual adventures with women. Eventually Baal kills Ekart in a jealous rage when his friend seems attracted by a waitress. Ultimately, Baal dies alone, wretched and afraid, deserted by his companions.

Brecht's first major work has its own poetic integrity and clearly transcends its original satiric intent. *Baal* is an unrestrained poetic statement about a chaotic, irrational, and self-destructive world and a celebration of the intense animal energy of its hero, who sees this world and calls it beautiful. Despite its satiric and grotesque comedy, *Baal* is a serious exploration of human experience, and the play demands close attention to its complex and dense poetic structure. It is obvious that Brecht satirizes the poet figure only on the most superficial level. The figure of Baal becomes the vessel for Brecht's own desires and fears, his own questioning of the nature of identity. In this first play, concerns are sounded and explored which were to direct a life's artistic work; and, despite its own vitality and intrinsic interest, *Baal* is significant primarily as a manifestation of the early Brecht's imagination in its initial grapplings with the major Brechtian themes.

Baal seems to be the manifestation of an acute despair. Brecht's early plays and poems testify to the anguish of his imagination. As this chapter discusses later, Brecht does celebrate the sexual vitality of his hero, but Baal is also presented as the victim of inevitable natural forces which direct his path to a lonely death. Baal is subject to a fierce, detached Nature in a frighteningly purposeless universe, and the strongest image in the play is that of a rotting corpse, slowly blackening in decay as it floats in the river under an empty sky. The vision of the early plays is, certainly, one held in a nihilist imagination. The relationship of the early Brecht to the primarily existentialist theatre of the absurd is increasingly clear. Brecht's early plays violate conventional form in a similar way to the absurdist drama because they both derive from a vision of a senseless universe in which man suffers an unredeemable isolation. In a limited way, I attempted to point out that similarity in an article comparing Brecht's *Im Dickicht der Staedte* (*In the Jungle of the Cities*) with Edward Albee's *The Zoo Story*.[3] Ralph Ley has done an excellent job of clarifying the existential attitude of the early Brecht in an article more directly concerned with this question. Ley uses Copplestone's definition of existentialism.

> In a passage depicting the area within which existentialism ought to be 'defined,' and reflecting to a considerable degree the young Brecht's own view of the cosmos as banefully influenced by the scientific revolution, Copplestone writes . . . of the rejection of Christianity and science by many people who 'find it difficult to believe in God. . . . [sic] The physical cosmos is alien to man in the sense that it is indifferent to man's ideals and hopes and strivings. It is not the geocentric, and indeed anthropocentric, cosmos of earlier days, but a vaster universe in which human existence and history appear as transitory and casual events.' After speaking of the apparent disintegration of the self in a world where man can find no 'final reassurance' and is forced to act, since man must, without the benefit of any principle of final casuality, Copplestone refers to him as 'alienated man, or man in a state of alienation,' in short the object of concern of both the existentialists and Brecht.[4]

To the young Brecht, Nature and human nature were something to be feared. Nature seemed to him to be more powerful than man—arbitrary, destructive, and irrational;

and human nature seemed even more frightening because of its use of the unconscious. To Brecht, the world was chaos, and—paradoxically—man both suffered that disorder and helped to create it. Brecht's nihilism grew from an acute sympathy for human suffering, and his response to that suffering is seen in the sense of isolation which directs *In the Jungle of the Cities*. In *Baal*, we find his imagination working in a confused attempt to clarify what human identity means in the chaos of this purposeless universe.

Most people, of course, will approach *Baal* from a knowledge of Brecht's later plays. The step backward from the powerful restraint of *Mother Courage* and the delicate charm of *The Caucasian Chalk Circle* to the violent explosion of poetic images in *Baal* provides an unexpected emotional assault. The far-reaching scope, in time and space, of this episodic structure provides no surprise to those familiar with the later Brechtian plays although this play lacks the clear structure of Brecht's major works in which the juxtaposition of scene against scene has clear and obvious significance. However, these loosely joined episodes are completely integrated in a thematic unity through the periodic invocations of the myth of Baal and the structure of the poetic imagery, an imagery which is not only violent and effusive, punctuated with iterative words, but richly textured with metaphor coloring metaphor. In fact, *Baal*'s full text is more dependent upon the structure of its poetic images than upon the visualization of its scene and action. This effusive imagery describes an unrestrained human nature—an instinctive energy which Brecht attempted to deny in his later Marxism.

Much of this rich imagery derives from the myth of Baal. Baal—with Dionysus, Persephone, and Osiris—shares the myth of a combat in the nether land and a return to life, the recurrent motive of death and resurrection which manifests itself in the seasonal pattern of the death of winter and the regeneration of spring. The sense of Baal as a god of fertility animates Brecht's play—most specifically in Baal's identification of himself with the seasons, the recurrent images of light and darkness, and the symbolic use of trees. Certainly the myth of Baal is

present in the "Chorale of the Great Baal" which precedes the actual play. Baal, from the canon of Canaanite
or Proto-Phoenician gods, is a god of the skies, storms, and
rains. Baal is a symbol of fertility; he is overcome in the
form of a bull in a sacrifice analogous to that of Dionysus.
With his death and the death of his son come barrenness,
the lack of vegetation of winter. The Ras Shamra text
reads: "Baal descends into the womb of the earth, when
the olive, product of the earth, and the fruit on the trees,
are subjected to the heat of the sun." [5] In the "Chorale of
the Great Baal," Baal descends to the earth, taking the sky
to cover his nakedness, and delights in sexual union with
"that girl the world." Baal's movement toward the earth is
a movement toward death.

> Baal eats all the grass and smacks his lips.
> When the fields are bare, Baal, singing, fares
> Into the eternal forests where he sleeps.
>
> When that girl the world begins to pull
> Baal down into darkness, what is she to him? He's full.
> And beneath those eyelids Baal has sky to spare:
> How could he use more now he lies there?
>
> In the dark womb of the earth the rotting Baal did lie.
> Huge as ever, calm, and pallid was the sky,
> Young and naked and immensely marvelous
> As Baal loved it when Baal lived among us. [6]

In the chorale, which is a poetic overture which introduces the primary motifs, the god, Great Baal, dies of
surfeit. Sated, he is unable to resist "that girl the world"
when she pulls him down into the dark womb of the
earth. In the play itself, after each of the heterosexual
experiences, the surfeited Baal experiences a disgust which
is usually manifested in some form of aggressive behavior
towards Emily, Johanna, or Sophie. The most intense
sexual disgust comes in the scene with the bum, when
Baal declares of women: "They are filth!" This disgust is
generated by the satisfaction of desire, and is, perhaps,
prompted by the same sense of revulsion that motivated
Shakespeare's later sonnets. In Sonnet 129, Shakespeare

presents a structure of sexual experience, projecting a movement from an irrational, uncontrollable energy to a state of sated revulsion.

> *The expense of spirit in a waste of shame*
> *Is lust in action, and till action, lust*
> *Is perjured, murderous, bloody, full of blame,*
> *Savage, extreme, rude, cruel, not to trust,*
> *Enjoyed no sooner but despised straight,*
> *Past reason hunted, and no sooner had,*
> *Past reason hated.*

In fact, the rhythm of the play is based upon the same progression of intense desire, acute sensation in gratification, and a temporary period in which the surfeited appetite revolts before the regeneration of desire. "I'm fed to the teeth!" is a recurrent declaration of Baal's surfeited appetite. This rhythmic structuring of the play in the pattern of appetite, consumption, satisfaction is further clarified in an interesting progression of images of light and darkness, a sequence which is first used in the chorale. In this poem, the color of the sky is dynamic, moving from "pallid" to "mauve" to "apricot" to the darkness of the night punctuated with "gloomy stars," and the degree of light in the poem moves from "the white womb" of Baal's mother to the "dark womb of the earth" in which the rotting Baal lies.

A consideration of these images of light and darkness reveals an interesting metaphorical scheme working in the play. In the second episode, Johannes' imagination sees a vision of the virginal "white body" of his beloved Johanna in a sexual embrace with a holly tree. Baal repeats the phrase, "white body," and throughout the play explores the quality of whiteness in his own erotic imagination: "She has white underwear round her body, a snow-white slip between her knees?" The rooms of Mech, which held Emily, were "white." "Beds . . . are white. Beforehand." Baal drops Emily "to the white clouds." The two young girls approach Baal's "broad and white" bed in the light. Baal declares to the landlady that he gorges himself "on white bodies." Ekart speaks of the "cathedrals with little white women," and he refers to himself and Baal as "two white doves." Baal sees the women who come to him as swans, and he defends his assault on Sophie by crying: "After all, it's spring. I had to have something white in this damned cavern! A cloud!" Later he says, "the air in this room is like milk. . . . You must have pale thighs." Immediately afterwards comes the scene in which the bum invokes the transfigured image of the "white body of Jesus" which is reminiscent of Baal's erotic vision of Johanna's white body. It is a Jesus who loves evil and who responds to the rotting dead dog with the comment: "It has beautiful white teeth." Baal says to Ekart that they must immerse themselves in blue water because the white roads threaten to hoist them, "like angels' ropes, into the sky." Reminiscent of the masturbating child of Baal's indecent cabaret song, Ekart describes a young woman's "soft white body" to Baal; and Baal decides to take Ekart's place with her at the willows at noon: "I'll simply satisfy her, the white pigeon . . . From here the clouds look beautiful through the willow branches."

From the isolation of these images, which represent only a sampling of the complete pattern, it seems obvious that the quality of light or whiteness is associated with the sexually appetizing: the desired object which attained and used moves from an unviolated and desirable whiteness to a darkness which itself moves from an ecstasy of darkness to a darkness associated with rotting, decaying flesh. In his description of love, Baal declares that love is like a coconut, good while it is fresh—and, correspondingly, white—bitter when the juice is gone and "you have to spit it out." Embracing Sophie under the trees, Baal listens to "the wild rushing of the wind in the wet black foliage." And he cries: "I am drunk and you are reeling. The sky is black, and we are on a swing with love inside us, and the sky is black." The image of white moving into darkness is also used to characterize the homosexual relationship of Baal and Ekart. Baal stops his male lover in the rain and says: "Here our white bodies can hibernate in black mud."

And when Baal wrestles with Ekart, in conflict with him because of his treatment of the pregnant Sophie, Ekart cries: "Do you hear what she says: in the undergrowth, and right now, it's getting dark? Degenerate beast! Degenerate beast!" However, the wrestling becomes an embrace, and Baal leads Ekart into the woods, after staring at the sky: "It's getting dark. We must camp out for the night. There are hollows in the wood where no wind penetrates."

The strongest image of this movement from whiteness to darkness is the figure of the white Johanna slowly rotting in her endless journey on the dark river. This image forces upon us the sense of mutability, the inevitability of violation and decay; it is combined with the sense of the body on the river submitting itself, passively, to the current and its restless journey. Ekart anticipates the action of Johanna's drowning, making it the typical action of those violated by Baal: "The women you have filled with your seed tumble into the black rivers." Rimbaud's violent and poetic imagery is a source for some aspects of the language of Brecht's Baal; and Willett discusses the possibility that Brecht's use of the image of the drowned voyager comes from Rimbaud's poem, *Le Bateau Ivre*, not only from the poem's recollection of waterlogged corpses but also from the sense of the body as passive object carried along by the river. Bernhard Blume also cites Rimbaud as Brecht's source, but finds Rimbaud's poem about Ophelia the specific source, putting Brecht and Rimbaud into the tradition of drowned-Ophelia poems.[7] No matter what the source, this grotesque image works to give *Baal* a pervasive sense of the deliquesence of life with the repetitious confrontation of the decomposed flesh of the young girl together with recurrent invocations of the river. Baal's song of "Orge's" glorification of the "john" is an outrageous variation of this basic image, relating the use of Johanna and the rotting of her corpse in the river to the process of the consumption of food and the production of excrement, a grotesque statement of the self-devouring Nature of the play.

Johannes and Johanna, both young idealists destroyed by Baal, almost seem to be the fragmentation of one character: one half who encounters Baal then dies, and decomposes in the river; the other half who encounters Baal and suffers a death in life. At the conclusion of the play Johannes sees the blackened, decomposed young girl, still floating on the river after seven years, in an image which combines the destructive movement of white to black with the image of consumption and surfeit:

> She's *still* floating. Nobody ever found her. Only I some-times have the feeling . . . that she is floating down my throat in all that brandy, a little small corpse, half rotten. And yet she was seventeen. Now she's got rats and seaweed in her green hair, it suits her quite well—a little puffed up, a little white, filled with stinking river mud, quite black. She used to be so clean. That's why she went into the river and got to be smelly.

Metaphorically, the river is both Baal himself and the irrational instinct to which he is subject. In this image, Johanna seems driven to the ironic action of washing herself in the river of sexual intercourse with Baal, ridding herself of her virgin cleanliness. Washing herself in the river is a metaphor for sexual embrace with Baal. In his imagination Baal washes himself clean in the sexual act; here the sexual act becomes a metaphor for the river. The river becomes a complex image: it is the strong energy of sexual instinct to which both Johanna and Baal must submit. In Johanna's experience, the river is Baal; and in Baal's imagination the current of the river is both his own instincts and some energy which is apart from him to which he must submit. This metaphor clarifies an impor-tant aspect of Brechtian thought: instinct, specifically sex-ual impulse, is seen as an element of being but, at the same time, something separate, something against which man must fight, something which attempts to control him and which he must deny. It is important, as well, to see that, in the world of Brecht's *Baal*, sexual instinct is not creative. The river is the place of decay.

While Baal has many Dionysian qualities, which certainly find their source in the parallel functions of Dionysus and Baal, the white bull of Phoenician myth, the play is not a celebration of the procreative function of Nature, represented in the progeny of man and the annual regeneration of the earth. The action is primarily devoted to Baal's fulfillment of his sexual urges; the lyrical response to that satisfaction celebrates acute sexual pleasure, not the promise of rebirth. In fact, several elements of the play work towards diminishing the sense of regeneration associated with sexuality. For example, Baal, himself, sees the pregnant female as an object of disgust; to Baal, pregnancy is not creative but degenerative.

> When summer swims off, mild and pale, they have already sucked up love like sponges, and they've turned back into animals, childish and wicked, with fat bellies and dripping breasts, completely shapeless, and with wet, clinging arms like slimy squids. And their bodies disintegrate, and are sick unto death. And with a ghastly outcry, as if a new world were on the way, they give birth to a small piece of fruit. They spit out in torment what once they had sucked up in lust.

Within the play there is reference to Baal as a god of fertility, as the source of seed. However, those women who are impregnated by Baal in the course of the play are subject to death, specifically drowning in the river—an image of the surrender to instinct which results in death; in one sense, then, the image of the river includes the concept of death and man's passive acceptance of it. Ekart describes the fate of Baal's female victims, a fate which is fulfilled in the suicides of Johanna and Sophie: "The women you have filled with your seed tumble into the black rivers." Related to the image of death in the river is the description of gradual decay, the inevitable withdrawal even from the promise of morning following night.

> *And the evening sky grew dark as smoke*
> *And held, when evening passed, the light suspended.*
> *In the morning brightness came again.*

There was night and morning even for her.

When her pale corpse rotted in the water
It befell that slowly God forgot her:
First her face; her hands then; then her hair.
In carrion-carrying rivers, she was carrion.

The recurrent images of rotting, which build upon the initial image from the "Chorale" of the god Baal himself, "rotting in the dark womb of the earth," work to emphasize mutability, not regeneration, putting stress upon the self-destructive quality of Baal's sexual energy.

In his introduction to *An Anthology of German Expressionist Drama,* Walter H. Sokel explains the presence of the motif of homosexuality in Bertolt Brecht's *Baal* and in modern literature in general as an attempt to express "the refusal to fit into any accepted pattern of behavior." [8] As such a violation of tradition, the motif joins others in the play's rejection of idealism. However, the homosexuality also functions to project the chaotic, self-destructive quality of Nature itself, for the temptation which Ekart provides for Baal is, essentially, a temptation to experience the general sensations which Nature provides in opposition to the specific pleasure provided by the female. When Baal is in the process of seducing Emily, he encounters Ekart's temptation:

> Baal! Let all that go! Come with me, brother! To the roads with their hard-caked dust and the air turning purple toward evening. . . . Come with me, brother! Dancing and music and liquor! Rain soaking you to the skin! Sun burning your skin! Darkness and light! Women and Dogs! . . . Come, brother Baal. Like two white doves, let us blissfully fly into the blue. Rivers in the light of dawn! Cemeteries in the wind! The smell of the endless fields before they are mown!

When several scenes later Baal deserts Sophie to join Ekart, he does seem to realize some positive relationship with Nature, ironically finding his perception of the pregnant sky beautiful in an attitude which contrasts strongly with his sense of revulsion for the pregnant woman:

Ever since, the sky has been greener, and pregnant, air of July, wind, no shirt in one's pants! They chafe my bare thighs. My skull's inflated by the wind. The smell of the fields clings to the hair under my armpits. The air's trembling, as if it had got drunk on brandy. . . . My soul, brother, is the groaning of the cornfields when they roll in the wind, and the glitter in the eyes of two insects that want to gobble each other up.

Baal's union with Nature is an accommodation of its chaos and self-destructive energy. It is in no sense a realization of the regenerative process. The Nature of *Baal* is not the "great creating Nature" of Shakespeare's romances. Neither does Baal in his accommodation of Nature's power over him share with Oedipus a sense of some higher form of order to which he is a patient, and Brecht provides no Colonus for Baal's assimilation into Nature. Rather Baal comes closer to Melville in holding the vision of God as the maw of universal death. Baal sees the created world as the dung of some cosmic digestive process.

BAAL   . . . I see the world in a mellow light: it is the Lord God's excrement.
EKART   The Lord God, who sufficiently declared his true nature once and for all in combining the sexual organ with the urinary tract!
BAAL   [*lying on the ground*]. It is all so beautiful.

Kant destroyed the notion of an empirically knowable universe with his declaration that the concept of order exists only in the mind of man and is an imposition upon the phenomenon of Nature whose source remains forever unknowable; and Schopenhauer widened the gap between man and Nature, an alienation which Darwin confirmed. Baal's acceptance of Nature is not a reconciliation of that estrangement. That acceptance has two sources: first of all, in Brecht's actual displacement of the myth of Baal, in which there is identification of the character with the elemental forces of the rain, the wind, and the sky; and, secondly, in the actual passive nature of Baal as a patient upon whom the forces of Nature act and who does not attempt to order or justify Nature within his own mind.

Baal is Baal with the greatest clarity at the moment of sexual climax when "in the fear and ecstasy of a created being, . . . [he becomes] God." However, Baal perceives himself acted upon in love by forces external to him.

> Love's like letting your naked arm drift in pond water with weeds between your fingers. Like torment at which a drunken tree, when the wild winds ride it, starts singing with a groan. Like drowning in gurgling wine on a hot day. . . . Your joints are pliable as plants in the wind. And the force of the attack is so great, you feel you're flying against a storm wind.

The analogy between Baal's image of love as an arm drifting in pond water, tangled in winds, and the image of the drowned Johanna, floating with the "seaweed and algae" making her heavier, is obvious. The Freudian implication of both love and death seen suspended in water is not as important, perhaps, as the clear association of love and death—both seen as forces like the river to which the floating voyager submits himself. Love to Baal is like the archetypal Biblical flood and in Brecht's imagery it leaves him and Johanna, after their sexual union, stranded on Mount Ararat.

Baal's identification of himself with the phenomena of Nature is a quality of the play's expressionistic form. Certainly, however, it is also something more. The tempest on the heath in *King Lear*, projecting the tormented consciousness of the king, is frequently discussed as an anticipation of Expressionism, employing the fragmentation of the individual into the objects or persons with whom he has contact. Two formal elements of Georg Kaiser's *From Morn to Midnight* show a clearer use of this fragmentation: the symbolic skeleton-tree in the third scene, which is a projection of the bank clerk's own realization of the presence of death, and the confessing sinners of the last scene who are aspects of the protagonist's own unrealized and inarticulated guilt. The process of appetite, gratification, and satisfaction is projected in Baal's recognition of the color of the sky, a recognition which is reinforced in the actual directions included in the text. However, in *Baal* this projection is not only the disintegration of the protagonist in a complex of characters and scenic elements, it is a displacement of the myth itself. Essentially, Baal is the presence of the sky and the fertility of the rain and, significantly, the force of the river. Baal seems to be the destructive energy of life itself.

One aspect of Baal's identification with Nature provides a recurring image of great power which is secondary only to the image of the drowned girl—that is the image of copulation with the tree. The development of this image belongs more to the homosexual episodes of the play than to the heterosexual. It is introduced in Johannes' erotic fantasy of Johanna with the holly tree and is developed in Baal's conception of the sexual embrace: "Just as the holly tree has many roots, all entwined together, so the two of you in the one bed have many limbs, and your hearts beat in your breasts and the blood flows in your veins." Later, after associating the barren trunks with filthy women, Baal cries in frustration at not being able to mate with trees and sublimates his desire by copulating with Sophie under the trees. When Sophie considers the time that she has spent with Baal, she anticipates her death in her imagination, thinking that her mother will consider her drowned; and Baal, associating himself, at this point, with the tree, says: "Three weeks, says the loved one in the roots of the trees, when it was thirty years. And at that very moment she had rotted half away." A striking recurrence of the image occurs in the beggar's anecdote about "a man who thought he was well. *Thought.*"—an anecdote told with a wry detachment more typical of the later Brecht. The man proceeds through the forest, the wilderness, to test his independence, which he discovers is not very great. At dusk, he confronts a large tree.

> He leaned against it, very close, felt the life inside it or thought he felt it, and said: you are higher than I, and you stand firm, and you know the earth below, and it holds you up. I can run and move better, but I don't stand firm, and

cannot go below and nothing holds me up. Also the great stillness above the treetops in the infinite sky is unknown to me. . . . The wind blew. A tremor ran through the tree. The man felt it . . . he threw himself down, embraced the wild, hard roots, and wept bitter tears. But he did that with many trees.

Baal asks: "Did he get better?" and the beggar answers: "No. But he died more easily." This anecdote, and Baal's own sexual response to the image of the tree, is answered in the song "Death in the Forest." Here the man, scorned by his fellows who see him as a mad Lear running naked on an eternal heath, clutches at the tree—an apparently typical action which evokes an empathetic response in the others:

> *Round him, round them, how the forest did roar!*
> *They heard him cry to the darkling sky*
> *And they could see how he clutched that tree*
> *And a shudder ran through them as never before.*
> *They trembled and clenched their fingers in a ball.*
> *For he was a man like them all.*

Baal, anticipating his own descent into earth to rot, continues the story of the man's cry to be a transparency for sun light and his eventual capture by earth, "who took him by his naked hand." The man is buried under the tree.

This song, a poetic elaboration of the beggar's anecdote, poses two problems in the play. First, it provides Baal's only response to his own experience in terms of being a member of a human community; it is Baal's only recognition of empathy. And, second, in the image which concludes the song there is a suggestion of transfiguration which is inconsistent with the sense of mutability which pervades the play. It is the only incident of light being regenerated from the thing buried.

> *And out of the thicket, and out of the night,*
> *They rode till, turning, they could espy*
> *That tree-grave towering toward the sky.*
> *And all of them wondered at the sight*

For the top of the tree was full of light.
They crossed their young faces and rode on
Into the heath and into the sun.

On one level, Baal's desired union with the tree and the equivalent fantasy of the death in the forest exist as sexual dreams, both the tree and the earth burial functioning chthonic symbols. On another level, these images work to define Baal's mythical progress in his journey from the sky to the womb of the earth. Earlier in the play, Baal uses this image to contrast his own exploitation of the trees with their use in Christian ritual. Baal sees the boughs nailed to the wall for the Corpus Christi procession as the bodies of women; and he holds Jesus, whose own union with the trees was accomplished on the cross, responsible for their murder: "the bodies of women which he nails to the wall, I wouldn't do that." The bum answers: "Nailed to the walls! They didn't drift down rivers, they were slaughtered for him, the white body of Jesus." Perhaps, the conclusion of "Death in the Forest" suggests a similarity between the mythical journeys of Baal and Jesus through the Christian references within the poem which anticipates Baal's own future.

There are many interesting ambiguities in *Baal*, but probably the most interesting complexity lies in the poet's response to Baal himself. Certainly, on one level the play is a celebration of Baal's extraordinary vitality, manifested primarily in his strong sexuality: a sexuality divorced from any sentimental commitments or ethical judgments, the pure animal enjoyment of immediate sensation. Baal demonstrates the kind of sexual freedom which Wedekind advocates, and Baal is the pure channel for sexual pleasure which the Marquis von Keith would like to be but which in him is dispersed in his financial and social manipulations. This pure sexuality is demonstrated in the first scene of *Baal*. After satisfying himself with food and wine, Baal becomes aware of Emily and grows sexually excited. He disregards any ethical commitment to the situation and makes lewd suggestions to her in front of her husband. He behaves this way regardless of the fact that her husband is the potential publisher of his poems. All of his energies are focused upon the satisfaction of his sexual desire; the ethical, financial, social consequences of his action are irrelevant to him. Even those senses which are not brought immediately into play are dulled; for example, his concentration upon her arms is so intense that he does not even hear the music she plays at the piano.

Except for the extended homosexual relationship with Ekart, Baal makes no commitment other than to the immediate experience. To Baal, relationships do not exist in time and space in recurrent patterns between recognizable personalities, because the only time which exists is now, and the only object external to Baal which is of any importance is the sexual object. Sokel speaks clearly on this point:

> His life is entirely of the moment. It makes no claims to continuity, and is therefore able to burn in undivided intensity. For this same reason, Baal's fascination for the men and women who are involved with him must always end in their disaster because the undivided life can only be a life for moments and cannot recognize duration.[9]

Baal himself does not recognize the continuity of personality. The flabby body of the pregnant Sophie, grotesque and distorted, bears no relation to the "something white," "the pale thighs" of the virgin original. The image of the drowned Johanna which haunts Baal might threaten this sense of fragmentation, perhaps. However, the image remains with him—haunts him—not through guilt, which would demand the continuity of act and consequence, but through Baal's increasing ability to articulate his vision of the world: "The Lord God's excrement." The vision of the drowned girl as carrion in "carrion-carrying rivers" is no manifestation of guilt; it is Baal's recognition of the "beauty" of the self-consuming universe. Baal declares that same vision in a more simply constructed metaphor at the beginning of the second episode:

> When you lie stretched out in the grass at night, you feel in your bones that the earth is a sphere and that we are flying

and that there are animals on this star eating up the plants.

Considering the question of ambiguity within Brecht's response to Baal, it is possible to recognize the play as a celebration of Baal's animal energy, an energy unfettered by ethical qualifications, a force which is committed only to its own satisfaction: "It's April. It's getting dark and you can smell me. That's how it goes with animals. And now you belong to the wind, my white cloud." Just as the elements of Nature with which the human Baal identifies himself, the natural phenomenon of Baal is not subject to any social contract. Certainly the poet Brecht rejoices in this freedom. Yet in a very real sense, Brecht presents Baal as far from free. Baal is Baal in a sexual experience—an experience which he sees as one in which he does not act but is acted upon—in the sense that he conceives of himself as the victim of his own instincts. Like his predecessor, Woyzeck, Baal is a passive hero who accepts the world, the forces external to his will, and is patient to them. Consequently, he—even more than Woyzeck— becomes an agent of destruction. Walter Weideli responds to this tension between vitality and destructiveness, outlining the Brechtian ambiguity:

> His hope is founded on despair. He imprisons man in the world here below and delivers him over to his fellows. Then too, there is a spontaneously dialectical intuition which links decay to existence and makes an effort to convert destruction into productive energy. . . . The young Brecht's hesitation is reflected in the contradictory relationships between himself and his heroes. He is not writing *Baal* to propose an ideal way of life for us, but rather to follow an experience through to its absurd conclusion. And if he is fascinated by the insolent vitality of the character, it is not without reserve.[10]

Part of that reserve according to Weideli, is contained in the "bitter irony" of Baal's lonely death: "He breaks down alone, calling in vain for the human presence he had so proudly pushed aside."[11] However, one would question Weideli's interpretation that Baal's final emotional condition is a state of despair generated by his sudden recognition of a failure to experience a single act of human communication. Baal is reluctant to die alone, yet his sense of "human presence" in this final scene is still defined in the metaphor of consumption. After he has been spit upon by one of his final companions, he asks another to wipe the spittle from his face, but he laughs because he likes the taste. The man calls him "You old gormandizer." He doesn't die, as Shlink of *In the Jungle of the Cities* dies, with an articulate realization of existential loneliness. Baal finds his existence defined in sexual sensation, in a relationship in which the object of desire is consumed; and he equates his experience of sexual satisfaction with his apprehension of the stars: "When I can't sleep at night, I look at the stars. That's just like the other thing." And when Baal finds himself dying alone, "alone again in my skin," he crawls out to the stars and dies. Baal's final movement is consistent with the metaphoric structure of the play and fulfills the Chorale which introduces the action:

> *Baal, he blinks at well-fed vultures overhead*
> *Waiting up among the stars till Baal is dead.*
> *Often Baal shams dead. So if the bird*
> *Falls for this, Baal dines on vulture, without a word.*

The ambiguity of his mother's "white womb," associated with the sky, and "the dark womb of the earth in which the rotting Baal did lie," complicates this final action. Baal moves from being the consumer to being that which is consumed. His final sensation derives from an erotic identification with the stars, the stars which contain the vultures who will now eat the corpse of Baal. The source of creative energy in Baal's world is an appetite which demands satisfaction, and its manifestation is "The Lord God's excrement," the created world.

Baal does exalt its grotesque hero's enormous sexual energy; however, within Brecht's ambiguous response to his hero, there is an implicit emphasis upon Baal as a destructive agent. While he is not explicitly judged, it is obvious that within the playwright's response to his hero, there is the seed of that later judgment which would qualify Baal's unrestrained enjoyment of Nature, essentially sexuality, in Mr. K.'s terms as a "diseased condition . . . something like a fever." [12] The probable originators of the myth of Baal bound together the fertility cult and the cult of the dead, and Brecht's association is an archetypal association. However, it is certainly significant to see that Brecht truncated the myth, both in the "Chorale of the Great Baal" and in the play itself: demonstrating the self-destruction of Baal's sexual energy without giving the promise of regeneration—asserting the nihilism upon which Brecht later built his polemic.

As I mentioned earlier, *Baal* does have a richness of language and action as a dramatic work which gives it an intrinsic interest and value. However, its primary significance remains its importance as a manifestation of the early Brecht's concern with the nature of human experience; and as this chapter has discussed that concern, two dominant themes assert themselves, consciously or unconsciously, in the text of this first play. First of all, Nature is seen as hostile, alienated from one aspect of man's being, a dynamic force to which man must submit; and, secondly, that force which demonstrates Nature's hostility is present in man himself within his own instincts. Instinct, at this point in Brecht's imagination, is part of that destructive energy of Nature. Esslin's description of the play in the appendix to his critical biography concludes with this remark: "[*Baal*'s] magnificently exuberant language expresses a passionate acceptance of the world in all its sordid grandeur." [13] In one way, one would agree with Esslin. Certainly, Brecht's structuring of Baal's action provides no explicit judgment of his hero. There is no sense in the play which indicates that Baal should have—or could have—acted differently. Brecht, as playwright, seems to accept the world, celebrate its vitality, and offers no alternative because, in this vision, there is no possibility for change. However, in the recurrent emphasis upon the metaphors of decay, the pervasive obsession with the natural process of the pure becoming the sullied, in the notion of the universe as a self-consuming animal—there is an implicit fear—a horror which is part of his fascination with this world but which is also an emotional response which qualifies that acceptance. In the early Brecht's conception of man, instinct is a destructive energy which destroys man; and yet man seems to affirm his identity only in sensual experience. In terms of this play, Baal is Baal only when he is engaged in some erotic activity; the moment, with its acute and immediate sensations, is supreme. Identity, in this conception, is not something which has continuity. Continuous and integral personality is not a factor of this world. In his "Prologue to Brecht's *Baal*," the German playwright Hofmannsthal senses the disintegration of the traditional concept of human personality which takes place in this play. The prologue takes the form of a group of players discussing the play. One of them comments: "The actor is the amoeba among all living things and therefore he is a symbolic man. The amoeba, that indeterminate primitive creature, which lets the situation dictate whether it should be animal or plant." [14] Early in this chapter the comment was made that the figure of the poet, Baal, seems to be the vessel for Brecht's own fears and desires. It seems to me that Baal's own recognition that his identity exists as he apprehends himself in sensation includes a latent fear that beyond sensation there is nothing. In that strange scene in the tavern with the Beggar, GooGoo, Bolleboll, and Maja, Baal reacts strongly to the absolute nihilism of "GooGoo's aria." GooGoo recites:

> The most beautiful thing is: Nothing. . . . It is like the trembling air on summer evenings. The sun. But it does not tremble. Nothing. Nothing whatever. One simply ceases. The wind blows, but one is no longer cold. It rains, one is no longer wet. Jokes happen, one does not laugh. One's body rots, one does not have to wait. General Strike . . . it is paradise. No wish remains unfulfilled. There is no wish left. You are cured of all bad habits. Even wishes. So you are free.

Of course, for all Baal's wild and unrestrained action, his freedom from ethical commitment, he is the passive victim of his own desires. He accepts Nature as it is manifested in his sexual energy, submitting to the river's current. The only freedom from this energy—and from Nature as a whole—is death. Paradoxically, Baal receives his identity through his acceptance of Nature; he is what Nature, the immediate environment determines, and he accepts those pleasures which are provided by the environment. When, weak with winter, he needs a woman as part of spring's regeneration of sexual desire, he seeks outside his door and uses the one available. However, Brecht's imagery includes the concept that submitting to Nature is a surrender to the process of decay; and as I mentioned earlier, the strongest image in the work is the image of Johanna floating down the river, slowly rotting. Accepting Nature is accepting the logic of decay and the ultimate loss of identity as you are consumed. Baal answers "Goo-Goo's aria":

> Swim down the river with rats in your hair:
> The sky will still be marvelous up there.
>
> . . . .
>
> Dance with wind, poor corpse, sleep with the cloud,
> you decadent God!

Baal's own death is prefaced by the lumbermen's predictions that he will be "stinking tomorrow," and—to them—he has ceased to be anything but a "pallid hunk" without even identification papers. This final scene is a repetitive chorus of the prediction of Baal's death, and the lumberman's words recall GooGoo's concept of the nothingness of death and Baal's own sense of the world as a flying sphere, to whose motion he must submit: "Don't be afraid: round as a ball the world will roll on. Tomorrow morning the wind will be whistling. Try to be more detached. Say to yourself: 'A rat is dying. So what?' Just take it easy." Deserted by his companions, Baal crawls toward the open door and the sky, whose vultures will consume him, committing himself to that universal digestive process, in which he will become part of the excrement of the created world.

2

In the Jungle of the Cities: The Isolation of the Human Soul

Recently critical attention has been directed to the early Brecht as a precursor of the Theatre of the Absurd. For example, in the introductory commentary to his edition of *Seven Plays by Bertolt Brecht,* Eric Bentley comments upon the submission of eros to the struggle for power in Brecht and Genet, and he notes analogies in the use of implicit homosexuality in Brecht's *Im Dickicht Der Staedte* (which he translates as *In the Swamp* rather than *In the Jungle of the Cities*) and Genet's *Deathwatch.*[1] In his study of Brecht, Martin Esslin declares that *In the Jungle* "anticipates the plays of Beckett, Ionesco, and Adamov, which it resembles by its insistence on the impossibility of communication."[2] Most recently, Walter H. Sokel has collected a group of expressionist plays which together form "A Prelude to the Absurd," and *Baal* is included in this *Anthology of German Expressionist Drama.*[3] The early Brecht shared his sense of the grotesque inexplicability of the world with the absurdists, and his early plays despair in an existential anguish. In charting the coordinates of the Brechtian world, it is necessary to explore the anguished sense of human isolation which cries out in the puzzling *In the Jungle of the Cities.* Of course, after experiencing the early plays of Beckett, Ionesco, and Albee, it is easier to reapproach *In the Jungle of the Cities* and understand its structure because we are more familiar with ways in which a sense of absurdity informs an imitation of human action. In a conscious and deliberate association, Brecht responded to the action of *In the Jungle of the Cities* as a boxing match, declaring that the essential conflict of the play should be judged as a boxing match with the skill or "style" of the opponents isolated for attention, not their motives for combat. In his forward, the playwright directs his spectators to witness the dramatic conflict in the same manner in which they would attend to a sporting event.

> You observe the inexplicable boxing match between two men. . . . Do not rack your brains over the motives for this fight but note the human stakes, judge without prejudice the style of each contestant, and direct your interest to the finish.[4]

In a boxing match it is the event itself which initiates the conflict, and the conflict is witnessed and judged on the basis of the fighter's immediate performance in competition. As far as the spectator's psychological evaluation of the event is concerned, the conflict is initiated out of stasis; and the resolution means this fighter is, at the conclusion of this event, victorious. In strong contrast to the dramaturgical construction of an Ibsen, a Strindberg, or a Hauptmann, Bertolt Brecht attempted here to project a dramatic metaphor of this arbitrarily initiated conflict, a conflict activated not out of aggression directed toward a specific individual, but rather a conflict activated out of stasis for the sake of the conflict itself. The spectator does not evaluate the present conflict in terms of the progressively complex situation of the past as he does in Ibsen and Strindberg, and to a lesser degree in Hauptmann; rather he focuses upon the event itself. And, primarily because of the fact that what is elemental about each combatant is realized in the fight itself, and is therefore unrelated to the sense of a motive developing in a specific and topical environment, the conflict is made more abstract and is, consequently, a bare and essential statement about man's relationship with man. Brecht's construction of a mythical environment, the Chicago of wild, irrational lawlessness, peopled with criminals and depraved parasites, forms a semi-wild West frontier town and a cosmopolitan metropolis where the son of a family from the plains—the savannahs—comes into conflict with a self-made lumber merchant, a Malayan born in Yokohama. Whether this grotesque parody held realism for the playwright or not, it provided him with a mythical scene in which the essential environment is not a recognizable reality but is rather man with man, the jungle of *the* cities in which man is seen as a commodity—purchased, consumed, and discarded.[5] Brecht's reconstruction assumes a surreality in which the significant elements are men.

As critics have noted, *In the Jungle* seems to prefigure the Theatre of the Absurd in its atmosphere of motiveless action. Martin Esslin suggests that the poetry of the absurd derives from its projection, in dramatic terms, of the poetic image—the dramatization of the metaphor.[6] However, *In the Jungle* remains one step from this projection; the playwright and the characters themselves use the metaphor to describe the action. And, while the action parallels the poetic image, the metaphor remains on the level of an image, and the action enjoys a separate life as a relatively mimetic presentation. The conflict is like a boxing match; but, at this point, the action and the metaphor are not the same thing. Brecht does not present Garga and Shlink in the boxing ring in the manner in which Beckett recently put his traditional triangle into concrete urns!

On the surface, the first scene of Brecht's strange play might seem to be Kafkaesque in the booklender's confrontation with a puzzling, apparently inexplicable adversary. However, Brecht is attempting to accomplish just the opposite sense: while Kafka's antagonists are manifestations of subconscious tensions generated in the psyche of the protagonist, Brecht's Garga is the arbitrary object of Shlink's desire to activate a conflict. The psyches of Garga and Shlink are always separate and recognizable.

Brecht schedules the conflict of *In the Jungle of the Cities* in two primary metaphors of possession: the action of sexual possession and the process of purchase and the subsequent claim of ownership. In this first scene, the emphasis is upon the former metaphor of possession, purchase. Shlink, surrounded by his parasites, enters the

rental library in which Garga is an employee, attempting
to purchase Garga's opinion of an arbitrarily selected
book: "I'm offering you forty dollars for your opinion of
this book, a book I don't know and that doesn't make any
difference." Shlink and his satellites balance the value of
the integrity of opinion against the potential value of the
money to Garga's deprived family and mistress, who live
in a squalid, reduced condition maintained by the inade-
quate salary earned by Garga. However, Garga even resists
the invocation of his dream of Tahiti, a dream of freedom
and comfort perpetuated in the Sunday illusions that he
and Jane Larry generate with their eighty-cent bottle of
whisky. Suddenly The Baboon brings in this Jane Larry
who has obviously been purchased herself, easily: "The
gentlemen are nice to me. . . . They bought me cocktails.
It's hot today, ninety-five degrees. It goes through your
body like a thunderbolt, George." The Baboon comments, "she has a body that's worth a few dollars. Can you
pay it, sir? It's a matter of love. It's a matter of cocktails."
Yet even when the price for his critical judgment is raised
to two hundred dollars, Garga refuses to sell. He exalts the
integrity of the mind by reading a passage from Rimbaud's A Season in Hell:

> Idolatry! Lies! Lechery! I am an animal, a Negro, but
> maybe I'm saved. You are fake Negroes, madmen, savages,
> misers! Merchant, you are a Negro, General, you are a
> Negro. Emperor, you old leper, you are a Negro, you drank
> untaxed liquor from Satan's factory. Oh, this people, in
> raptures about fever and cancer!

Here Garga uses the commonplace inversion that there is
greater freedom in slavery than in authority, a state of
responsibility in which the individual has to make commitments to external standards. Garga's departure at this
point is an attempt to return to the wild, uncivilized,
precommitted state: " 'I am unschooled in metaphysics,
do not understand the laws, have no morals. I'm a wild
man. You are wrong.' " Garga accompanies this speech
with the action of stripping off his clothes, which to him

seem to act as symbols of his identity with Shlink's world in which a man can become a commodity. However, the integrity of Garga's soul has now been put to question; Shlink has gotten "under his skin," and the boxing match has begun.

In the second scene, Garga himself begins to fight. The match has been scheduled, so to speak, and there seems to be no question of his participation. However, his style of combat, at this point, is to act as patient to the action of Shlink, to receive passively what the Malayan imposes upon him. He says: "I'm the Negro in this. I came with a white flag, and now I unfurl it for an attack." In a kind of submission, Garga dresses in the clothes provided for him by Shlink, the uniform of his parasites. This action reverses the symbolic stripping of the first scene. This second scene is constructed upon an amazing play of dominance and submission which directs Garga and Shlink to make ambiguous gestures which are at the same time exertions of power and passive accommodations of the energies of the other. It is probably these ambiguous gestures to which Eric Bentley is referring when he discusses the "negative dynamics" of *In the Jungle*.[7] For example, Garga's submission to Shlink's scheme of the transfer of ownership of the lumber business forces him to become a figure of authority, deciding upon the fate of the business and its employees. At the same time Shlink, who has initiated the conflict, also battles through submission:

> My house is yours, this lumber business belongs to you. From today on, Mr. Garga, I place my fate in your hands. I don't even know you. From today on I am your creature. Every glance from your eyes will disturb me. Each one of your wishes, even those I don't know, will find me willing. Your cares are my cares, my strength will be your strength. My feelings will be dedicated to you alone, and you will be angry.

Shlink's aggression, the energy of his will, is manifested in what appears to be an act of surrender to Garga; and the implicit sexuality of this action is seen in the language of surrender which becomes the language of the lover, wooing the loved one in the words of consummate dedication to his pleasure and comfort. By becoming Garga's benefactor—endowing him with money, an equation for power—Shlink attempts to dominate Garga through obligation.

In this play of dominance and submission, the question of identity is certainly a significant one. Shlink's submission to Garga realizes itself in witnessing, to a degree, the recreation of his own identity in Garga: Garga the booklender becoming Garga-Shlink the lumber merchant. And while Garga maintains that "A new skin compensates for nothing," his relative metamorphosis from a passive man to an aggressive agent belies his statement. He becomes the irrational holder of power, destroying the business by scheduling a double sale and placing the loyal employees in a state of poverty. Working within the equation of money and power, Shlink has created the new Garga with an act of his own will, the transfer of power. Garga himself recognizes the recreation:

> When I came here, I'd been skinned—right down to the bone. I'm trembling from two weeks of spiritual debauchery. I spit in his face: many times. He swallows it. I despise him.

The rationale of Garga's argument with his sister, Marie, whom he refuses to help when she is forced into the prostitute's role, defines his own loss of integrity. Implicit in his argument is the fact that an individual is what he does; that identity cannot be separated from behavior: "[what you want is] to seek bread for your parents in a whore's bed. And to sell the stink of horses and say: this isn't me!" The purchase of Marie helps to define the parallel action of Garga's purchase; he realizes that she is being treated like an article of food, to be bought for consumption: "You like it at the market? . . . now a few pounds of flesh are up for auction!" Immediately after this recognition, Garga himself, acting under the power given him by Shlink, accomplishes a grotesque imitation of

Shlink's attempt to purchase his integrity. Garga "sells" the property of the lumber business to a young man from the Salvation Army for the freedom of spitting in his face. At first the man refuses; but since his membership in the Army commits him to altruism, he must submit, and eventually he suffers a false suicide from his humiliation.

Brecht's vision of the universe as a self-devouring being pervades his first play, *Baal*, and with *In the Jungle of the Cities* he again applies the image of consumption to the action of man's exploitation of man. The tragedy of this play lies in the fact that even in the act of consumption, which reduced to essential terms is sexual usage, the human being remains alone, incapable of communicating with the other one.

However, Shlink's attempt to achieve contact with another human being, his activation of the boxing match — to use Brecht's metaphor — does initiate an irreversible sequence of events in which both participants are inextricably bound. Garga himself says

> A certain man insults another. That is unpleasant for the latter. But a certain man under certain circumstances will pay a whole lumber business to insult another. That is, of course, even more unpleasant. In such cases, the insulted man ought to leave town, but since it might be too pleasant, maybe even that is no longer possible for him.

Garga claims that he is free; yet he immediately denies his freedom, explaining how the submission to habit, like coffee-drinking, and the commitment to another individual in the acceptance of sacrifice, insure his lack of freedom: "when a man is grown, and wants to do something and give it everything, he finds he is already paid for, initiated, certified, sold at high price. And he is not free to go under." The inevitable consequence of the conflict which Shlink originates assumes, partially through its inexplicability, the awesomeness of the inevitability of tragedy. Northrop Frye clarifies this sense of tragic inevitability in *Anatomy of Criticism* with his discussion of Adam as the archetype of the tragic hero.

Adam, then, is in a heroic situation: he is on top of the wheel of fortune, with the destiny of the gods almost within his reach. He forfeits that destiny in a way which suggests moral responsibility to some and a conspiracy of fate to others. What he does is to exchange a fortune of unlimited freedom for the fate involved in the consequences of the act of exchange, just as, for a man who deliberately jumps off a precipice, the law of gravitation acts as fate for the brief remainder of his life.[8]

The ultimate consequence of Shlink's attempt to purchase Garga is his own consumption. His initiation of the conflict in the state of stasis is an assertion of his own freedom, but once that freedom is asserted it no longer exists and he, himself, is subject to the logic of consumption, the process of one individual feeding upon another. *In the Jungle* and *The Measures Taken* are ironic reversals of the same coin. The Young Comrade submits himself to the logic of the loss of identity in the act of ultimate altruism just as Shlink accepts the logic of the act of devouring Garga. And yet, in the very ambiguity which is the nature of tragedy, the conflict itself generates the real vitality of the participants; and in the conflict, both Shlink and Garga, while unable to achieve contact, gain an acute awareness of their own isolated identity—a recognition which kills Shlink and completes the initiation of Garga.

The implicit homosexuality of the initial scenes becomes explicit as the conflict progresses.[9] Perhaps, the sexual ambiguity of Garga is further defined by an expressionist fragmentation of character into male and female, Garga and Marie. This division recalls the earlier sexual fragmentation of Johanna and Johannes in *Baal*. Garga is bound to Shlink in a strong attraction, but it is possible that the attraction is clarified in Marie's acute desire for the Malayan lumber merchant. In her desire and its fulfillment, she grows aware of herself as an object for consumption; Shlink tells Garga: "You have opened her eyes to what she'll be among men forever and forever: an object." In the scene in which her love for Shlink is consummated, Marie sees the trees, the traditional symbol of verdure and fertility, "draped with human dung," the excrement of consumed food. The actual union takes place while Manky describes the fate of Marie the prostitute in images of consumption:

> The bitch will be swallowed with her skin of feathers, digestion will be accelerated by prayers, vultures will be shot according to martial law.

Returning to the stage after the consummation of their love, Marie claims that Shlink acted as if he were taking her in sacrifice; and Shlink responds to Marie's action as that of a mad bitch. Marie completes the association of sexual possession and commercial purchase: "I love you like a mad bitch. . . . But now pay me. Yes, I'd enjoy being paid. Give me your bills, I want to live on the money. I'm a whore."

In the metaphysical context of *In the Jungle* love is an irrational animus, an all-encompassing passion which focuses all the human energies into the achievement of the object. Consequently, Garga and the man in Manky's anecdote ignore their family's need, Marie dismisses the ethical, social, and physical consequences of her life as a whore, and Shlink destroys his life's work: all in an inevitable submission to the animus of their sexual passion which, satisfied, achieves no more than "warmth from bodily proximity." The entire course of *In the Jungle* works to deny the romantic idealization of sexual love. Just as the love of Marie for Shlink is answered in the commercial sale of her body in the dung-draped forest, the traditional *gamos* is ironically celebrated in the wedding feast of Garga and Jane Larry—the feast of a criminal and a whore; and the apex of sexual love in *In the Jungle* is homosexual.

As the play develops, the metaphor of possession in purchase and use becomes even more frequently associated with the metaphor of possession in sexual union. Scene V begins in a contrapuntal presentation of these images in three variations—each dealing with a separate surrender to passion. Manky tells his anecdote about a man who used a sum of two thousand dollars, not to save his starving family, but to purchase the use of a certain woman's body, which he could possess in no other way. His sexual appetite destroyed his sense of responsibility to his family, and the desertion of this man in the anecdote certainly suggests Garga. The Baboon tells the story of Shlink who, "through passion," lost his business and is reduced to carrying coal. And The Worm describes Shlink as a "worn-out race hound" and Garga as his irresistibly attractive "little bone." Garga conceives of himself as the whore-wife of Shlink.

> 'In my dreams I call him my hellish husband—that dog, Shlink. We are parted from bed and board, he hasn't got a room. His little bride smokes Virginia cigars and earns something to put in her stockings.' That's me. '. . . Some day I shall be his widow. Surely the day has already been marked in the calendar. And I shall walk in clean underwear behind his corpse, my legs spread good and wide in the warm sun.'

Garga has conquered Shlink through his sexual attraction. Shlink says: "The conquerors of the world like to lie on their backs." Here the physical attitude of submission defines Garga's relationship with the older man when Garga immediately goes into the bedroom, lies down on the bed and says: "My back wears thin as a fishbone from lying down." Shlink's voice then assumes the tone of a lover: "Laugh! I love your laughter. Your laughter is my sunshine, it was miserable here before. What grief not to see you! It's been three weeks, Garga."

The image of consumption extends beyond sexual exploitation into Garga's conception of Shlink devouring his whole identity: "What is human for me, you swallow it like so much meat. You open my eyes to some new source of supply precisely by stopping it up. You make my own family into a source of supply. *You* live on *my* resources! And I grow thinner and thinner. Now I am getting into metaphysics! And yet you dare to vomit all this up in my face!" Shlink's domination of Garga includes the gradual but pervasive integration of himself into Garga's family. He supports the family by carrying coal—consuming Garga's identity by usurping his function. And, in the complex play of identity and obligation, when Shlink is arrested for the double sale of lumber ordered by Garga, Garga himself submits to the arrest and a three-year imprisonment. Garga accomplishes this action to balance the obligation and destroy his enemy: "now I'll liquidate all: I'll draw a line under our account, and then go . . . I, I am slaying my enemy . . . And I'd still like to see your real face, Shlink, your milk-white, damned invisible face."

In an arbitrary plot-device, Garga plans to publish an accusation of Shlink just before he is to be released from his imprisonment:

> To the Police. I wish to direct your attention to the Malayan lumber dealer, C. Shlink. This man has pursued my wife Jane Garga and seduced my sister Marie Garga, who was in his service.

Garga promises: "For him the day of my release will be marked by the howling of the lynch gang."

When he is released from prison and confronts Shlink, a meeting which does take place against the screams of the lynching gang, Garga claims that he is no longer consumed by the passion which dragged him down. However, when Shlink cries: "Come with me!", he repeats his submission. The match is not yet ended.

Within the play the two primary rituals of sacrifice and initiation are implicit. While much of the attention is focused upon Garga, it is Shlink, the Malayan lumber merchant, who is the central tragic figure. It is Shlink who makes the free choice, the decision to devour Garga, and he is subject to the logical conclusion of that act, his own consumption. Shlink's tragic action is generated in what Garga calls "the black mania of this planet—the mania for contact." However, the experience of contact remains impossible, even in enmity. Here Brecht denies even the contact attempted in sadistic sexual relations, the realization of contact in pain. In his three-week battle with

Garga in the gravel pits of Lake Michigan, Shlink experiences a tragic realization in an image of the acute solitude of man:

> The endless isolation of man makes even of enmity an unattainable goal. Even with animals it is impossible to come to an understanding. . . . If you stuff a ship with human bodies till it bursts, there will still be such loneliness in it that one and all will freeze. . . . Yes, so terrible is the isolation that there isn't even a fight.

The focus of Shlink's energy transcends mere sexual pleasure; this focus centers upon the acute need to experience communion with some thing external to his own self. But instead of communion, he experiences only the awareness of proximity: "Love—warmth from bodily proximity—is our only grace in all the darkness. But the union of the organs is the only union and it can never bridge the gap of speech." In Christian terms, the object of the search for that which is external to the consciousness is God and the achievement of that object is Grace. In Shlink's world, there is no God and no promise of Grace other than the comforting sense of warmth from another body, existing in its own isolation. Jacob wrestled with the stranger and saw God face to face in a contact manifested in the touching of his thigh. However, for Shlink the gravel pits near Chicago provide no Peniel, and the wrestling with Garga no communion.

Shlink's tormented realization of the "gap of speech" anticipates Ionesco's sense of the tragedy of language and is even more concretely answered in Hamm's progressive withdrawal from all which is external to his own consciousness in Beckett's *Endgame*. Here the final renunciation is the denial of speech: "Let's play it that way and speak no more about it . . . speak no more . . . Old stancher! . . . You . . . remain." In Brecht's play the isolation is mimetically represented in Garga's actual departure; in Beckett's play the isolation of the human condition is more abstractly projected, and Clov need not depart: the isolation is complete even with his presence.

The ritual of initiation frequently informs drama in the imitation of a character's transition from innocence to experience, from idealism to realism. Garga's initiation within *In the Jungle* is precisely stated. He moves from the idealistic cry of freedom in Rimbaud's words and the illusion of primitive freedom contained in the image of Tahiti to the knowledge that freedom is unattainable. The image of Tahiti is also associated, significantly, with the regressive fantasy of retreating from the world and establishing an idyllic home with his mother. But Garga rejects Tahiti and moves toward New York—from the jungle of Chicago to the more complex jungle of New York. His initiation equips him with a vision equivalent to that of Shlink: the realization that the conflict itself, the search for contact prior to the knowledge that contact is impossible, is the primary value. Holding the money, the symbol of power, standing as successor to the tragic Shlink, Garga declares: "To be alone is a good thing. The chaos is used up now. It was the best time."

In the Jungle presents an even more frightening world picture than that projected in *Baal*. True, the image of the universe as a self-devouring creature dominates both plays; but in *Baal* the elementary force, sexual energy, is celebrated as vital in spite of its grotesque and destructive nature. The magnificence of Baal is undeniable. There are obvious parallels between Baal and Shlink; one looks like a Malayan and the other is. But Shlink is another being. What is vital in *Baal* is debilitating in *In the Jungle*. That which Baal destroys seems sacrificed to super energy. Shlink's passion enervates and gradually consumes, disintegrating in a pervasive and irreversible decay. In these two early plays the primary energy is sexual; however, in the unrelieved and malicious destructiveness of *Baal* and the isolation of the human soul of *In the Jungle*, we have seen that within this celebration one part of the poet judges that the free exercise of instinct is an evil thing. However, in *Baal* and *In the Jungle*, Brecht's characters are allowed no ethical choice: the tragic vision does not contain the opportunity to decide. *Baal*, the play, and

Baal, the character, are particularly significant because they project Brecht's tragic vision in his primary image of the irrational stream of life in which man, the helpless patient, is hopelessly caught up. The earlier discussion of *Baal* demonstrates that Brecht's vision of the universe was determined by the metaphor of the river and that the concept of the passive acceptance of Nature is contained in the symbolic action of the character floating, submissively, upon the river under the dynamic changes of the sky. *Baal* and some of the poems from the *Hauspostille* seem to derive from an attempt to achieve an identification with the beauty and the vitality of this vision of Nature. In the final stanza of the poem, "Of Swimming in Lakes and Rivers," Brecht constructs an image of complete surrender to the river, the abnegation of all personal energy and the achievement of total inertia, accepting the support and motion of the river. The action described seems almost to be a mystic atonement with Nature.

> *You must, of course, lie on your back quietly*
> *As is usual and let yourself go on drifting.*
> *You must not swim, no, but only act as if*
> *You were a mass of flotsam slowly shifting.*
> *You must look up at the sky and act as if*
> *A woman carried you, and it is so.*
> *Quiet, without disturbance, as the good God himself does*
> *When at evening he swims in his rivers here below.*[10]

The image of floating in the womb is, of course, the ultimate metaphor of this patient acceptance of nourishment, protection, and anonymity. However, this celebration of Nature is not a lyrical response to the beauties of the world. Brecht's Nature contains its beauties, but it is primarily a fierce, hungry universe, a grotesque organism feeding and producing excrement:

> *Toward morning the fir trees piss in the gray light*
> *And their vermin, the birds, begin to cheep.*[11]

Nature in the poems from the *Hauspostille* is a disgusting being. "Song on Black Saturday at the Eleventh Hour of the Night before Easter" contains Brecht's personal identification with this destructive Nature in the sense of the poet, as macrocosm, containing its disgusting processes:

> *The wind blew—more swiftly through my walls,*
> *And still it snowed. It rained in me.*

> *The mean snouts of cynical fellows have discovered*
> *That in me nothing at all exists.*
> *Wild swine have paired in me. Often in me*
> *Out of milky heavens ravens have pissed.*[12]

Nature in these poems is a devouring force; it is the "boughs, thick as a man's arm, knotty" which bury Cortez' men:

> *Slowly the forest*
> *Under the strong sun while a light wind blew,*
> *Silently, in the next weeks, ate the meadows up.*[13]

And Nature is the flood water which drowns the men of Fort Donald in the woods, "pitiless and blind." [14] Nature is sickness, deprivation, suffering in opposition to the quiet sleep and protection of the womb which seems to provide the only security and comfort man can know. Nature is also "the coldness of the woods" which, Brecht felt, even penetrated the security of his mother's womb:

> *I, Bertolt Brecht, come from the black forests.*
> *My mother carried me to town while in her womb I lay*
> *And still the coldness of the woods lingers*
> *And shall remain in me until my dying day.*[15]

Within this vision of the universe the submission to an irrational, destructive force is the typical human action. It is extremely significant that Brecht allows the characters from his early poems and plays no opportunity to reject the force present in the image of the river. Even in his fantastic strength, brutal egoism, and sexual energy, Baal is controlled by irrational forces—the irrationality of Nature and the irrationality of his own nature. The image of man subject to moving, chaotic force, which in the poem, "Ballad of Mazeppa," is a fatal ride strapped on the back of a wild horse, is seen as the primary image of *Baal*. Baal sees himself hurtled through the universe: "you feel it in

your bones that the earth is a sphere and that we are
flying." In the image with which he describes his submission to sexual love, Baal associates himself with the body
of Johanna floating endlessly on the river, growing from
white to black, slowly decomposing. And in "Orge's
Song," man himself becomes the vessel for the process of
consumption, satisfaction, and decomposition. On the
"john," man becomes the image of that process.

> It is a place where you rejoice to know
> That there are stars above and dung below.
>
> .   .   .   .
>
> A place of wisdom where one has the leisure
> To get one's paunch prepared for future pleasure.
> And there you find out what you are indeed:
> A fellow who sits on a john—to feed! [16]

Baal sees the world as "The Lord God's excrement." It is
the universe ironically exalted in "Grand Chorale of
Thanksgiving."

> Praise ye the grass and the beast which neighbor you, living
>   and dying.
> Behold, like to yours
> Is the life of the grass and the beast,
> Like to yours must be their dying.
> Praise ye the tree which groweth exultant from carrion unto
>   heaven!
> Praise ye carrion,
> Praise ye the tree that ate of it
> But praise ye the heavens likewise. [17]

With In the Jungle of the Cities Brecht concentrates
upon the realization that inside this chaotic and irrational
universe man exploits and consumes his fellow man, attempting to achieve some sense of communion, but that
this contact is impossible. In its total isolation, the human
soul can touch only itself. This same realization directs
the final stanza of the ironic hymn of praise:

> Praise ye from your hearts the unmindfulness of heaven!
> Since it knoweth not

Either your name or your face,
No one knoweth if you are still there.

Praise ye the cold, the darkness and corruption!
Look beyond:
It heedeth you not one jot,
Unmoved, you may do your dying.[18]

On a social level, this concept of the self-consuming aspect of Nature takes the form of the exploitation of the other person in the attempt to gain sexual pleasure. The human being in *In the Jungle* is treated as a commodity, purchased and used. One of Brecht's strongest images of exploitation is found in the "Legend of the Dead Soldier," which Martin Esslin calls "the first characteristically Brechtian poem." [19] This poem was generated in Brecht's wartime experience, in his confrontation with the wounded and the dead which his work as a medical orderly demanded. In this grotesque poem the dead soldier is dug up, and the medical commission declares him fit for service again. The decomposing body of the dead soldier is paraded through the streets in preparation for his return to the front—to provide a target for the enemy once more.

The medical commission trailed out
To the little acre of God
And with sanctified spades they dug the fallen
Soldier out of the sod.

. . . .

With fiery schnapps they tried to rouse
His rotted limbs to life.
They hung two nurses on his arms
And his half-naked wife.

And since the soldier stank of rot
A priest limped on before
Who waved an incense burner about
So he should stink no more.[20]

This poem vividly demonstrates the poet's acute compassion for human suffering. This suffering is all the more cruel and meaningless because it takes place in a godless world. It is important to realize that these early poems and plays are essentially works of religious despair. In Brecht's world, there is no beneficent God witnessing the actions of the earth; the heavens are empty, and only the stars look down upon the gruesome sight of the dead soldier paraded through the streets. In the "Grand Chorale of Thanksgiving" Brecht cries ironically: "Praise ye from your hearts the unmindfulness of heaven!" It is the separation of human suffering from any cosmic purpose which makes necessary our compassion.

In the early poems and plays Brecht explores the human consciousness, attempting to define itself in terms of that which is outside of itself. In *Baal*'s metaphysics, Brecht reaches the conclusion that man is the victim of Nature. In the final scene, Baal commits himself to this devouring Nature, but with a pathetic regret that he is dying alone. With *In the Jungle of the Cities* Brecht perceives the human consciousness attempting to define itself in terms of a relationship with another human being; and, in the acute suffering of the protagonist as he experiences a tragic recognition, Brecht seems to conclude that man is unable to reach communion with another human soul even in the intimate proximity of a sexual relationship. Communion with another human being is the dream; the reality is exploitation and consumption as the other becomes either an object for sexual use or a devouring agent itself. Within *In the Jungle* Shlink attempts to assert his will. Brecht regards his encounter with Garga as motiveless, and critics interpret the action as *acte gratuit*. In rational terms, surely, this encounter is inexplicable; and yet, as Baal must exploit and consume other human beings because that is human action, so Shlink must reach out and consume. However, Shlink attempts, through his own will, to reach out and experience another human being. In his attempt to realize, in his own consciousness, a sense of another person as more than an object, he can only initiate a sexual relationship in which he uses the other person. He can extend himself toward another only by imposing his own identity upon him and assuming the other's identity. Even this sensual exchange of identities is fruitless and unsatisfying, and succumbing to the natural law of consumption, Shlink dies, used and assimilated by Garga who has learned that exploitation is the only course in this hostile and inexplicable world. Garga accepts the natural law of consumption, submitting to Nature. Brecht's own response to human suffering informs these plays and poems, and that anguished isolation is more painful as its compassion seems futile. These plays are imitations of an event which becomes the essential action for Brecht: the vain struggle of a human consciousness to exert its own will in a hostile world. That struggle becomes, in Brecht's dramatic disguises, the submission of the individual will to some energy which exists apart from it. This conception of human action could be discussed in terms of a dramatic tension as well, since it is the exploration of a dialectic. In these terms, then, the primary tension is Brecht's sense of man as agent, capable of determining action, and man as patient, victim of forces external to him. Esslin describes this tension as a conflict between reason and instinct.

> Brecht's passive acceptance of incomprehensible emotional forces was counterbalanced by an increasingly strenuous effort at rational, active self-control. Gradually the passive submission to instinct was resisted and gave rise to feelings of guilt and distaste.[21]

The complications in Esslin's perceptive definition of the conflict in Brecht's poetry come in the fact that, with some frequency, the rational assumes the quality of the instinctive. In *A Man's a Man*, for example, reason would argue that Galy Gay's assimilation into the collective is a good thing. At least it provides a rational way out of the trouble into which he has fallen; and his new identity has greater functional value and social strength even though he seems less free. As this study of Brecht discusses somewhat later, the Army, as metaphor for Brecht's sense of the collective, assumes some of the same metaphoric qualities as Nature. The less equivocal image of the collective,

The Party, in *The Measures Taken* devours individuality, consuming the body of The Young Comrade in the lime pit, in a way which relates it—surely unconsciously—to the Nature of the earlier poems and plays. Of course, this conflict informs much of the actual discussion which follows. But it is important to note it at this early point so that it is possible to approach these plays with a fuller understanding of this essential conflict. As Bentley declares, there is a remarkable integrity in Brecht; and certainly it is most profitable to read these later and master plays of Bertolt Brecht as fuller, more complex, and more intricately displaced reworkings of this initial search for identity in a hostile world in which the human will is subject to strong and irrational energies, both from within and without.

Recall that Esslin's statement of the essential conflict states that Brecht's work demonstrates an "increasingly strenuous effort at rational, active self-control." We see that control starting most obviously in *A Man's a Man*. In a sense, the exploration of the nature of the human will in the earlier plays is a less conscious—and, consequently, more honest—manifestation of the playwright's imagination. With the development of the conventional Brechtian dramatic structure, there is the implication of a rational control upon the creative process itself, or so it seems. In *A Man's a Man*, for example, Brecht schedules the conflict so that the force which is in opposition to the individual will, in this case the energy of the collective, is given some value as rational. And the instinctive energy of sexuality is punished, even "plucked out" in the self-castration of Sergeant Fairchild; and while this act is seen ambiguously and is destructive, it is within the given fictional ethic, rational. The ironies in this play are confusing, but, as the next chapter discusses, the play is transitional, coming between the pure and almost freely undisplaced explorations of Brecht's central nihilistic myth of human action and the conscious attempts to relate this to the positive doctrines of Marxist humanism.

3

A *Man's a Man:* Identity and the Collective

A *Man's a Man* marks the beginning of that particular dramatic style which we recognize as Brechtian. The earthy humor, the exaggerated projection of social relationships, and the improvisational quality of comic action are anticipated in the earlier plays; but in A *Man's a Man* they form a consistent dramatic structure for the first time. The episodic plot becomes a sequence of comic turns as well as an organically organized poetic structure. However, the primary difference between this comedy and the dramatic outcries which precede it seems to derive from a difference in the playwright's attitude toward human experience and its imitation in art. With A *Man's a Man,* Brecht appears to assume a more detached attitude, and from this point on the plays seem to change from being direct manifestations of anguish to being more rational, objective explorations of the specific and local conditions which cause that anguish. Eric Bentley writes:

A NEW BRECHT.
The protagonists of the earlier plays—Baal, Kragler, and Garga—were mouthpieces for Brecht's own yearnings and agonies. We are still not as far as he liked to think from the agonized-ecstatic dramas of the Expressionists. With A *Man's A Man* emerges the Brecht the world knows. The transition is rather an abrupt one, and I wonder that more has not been made of it. Formally speaking, it could be taken as a switch from tragedy to comedy. Brecht's final attitude would be vehemently anti-tragic. The new-fangled notion of Epic Theatre can be construed as a synonym for traditional Comedy.[1]

Bentley has clearly identified the shift in the playwright's perspective which is evident in the assumption of a comic attitude. The development of this attitude does not necessarily mean that Brecht had accepted the conditions of human life against which he cried out in the earlier plays. However, the wry detachment and the more objective exploration suggest that he was able to come to terms with his despair. In *Baal* and *In the Jungle of the Cities*, Brecht seems to despair of the helpless state of man who is subject to the irrational forces of Nature, including the chaos of his own human nature. Baal, Shlink, and Garga are not agents in the sense that they are able to assert a will; rather they suffer the irrational energy of human instinct. While the playwright's strong compassion is clear in these plays, they seem to derive from a hopeless conception of man. *A Man's a Man*, in its ambiguity, contains some of the same despair. In one sense, Galy Gay is clearly the passive hero acted upon by forces external to him. But there is one strong central fact present in this text; a fact which dominates Brecht's work from this point on—the possibility of human change—"You can do with a human being what you will. Take him apart like a car, rebuild him bit by bit." [2] Before we examine the quality of this transitional play, it would be helpful to consider Brecht's own attitude toward it, exploring the implications of the following statement made by Brecht as an introduction to a radio broadcast of the play. Brecht begins his statement with a declaration that human society itself is in transition and that the products of the old humanity—aesthetic and technical—no longer have vitality and significance for man.

> This stratum of humanity had its great period. It created monuments that have remained, but even these remaining monuments can no longer arouse enthusiasm. The great buildings of the city of New York and the great discoveries of electricity are not of themselves enough to swell mankind's sense of triumph. What matters most is that a *new human type* should now be evolving, at this very moment, and that the entire interest of the world should be concen-

trated on his development. The guns that are to hand and the guns that are still being manufactured are turned for him or against him. The houses that exist and are being built are built to oppress him or to shelter him. All live works created or applied in our time set out to discourage him or to put courage in him. And any work that has nothing to do with him is not alive and has nothing to do with anything. This new human type will not be as the old type imagines. It is my belief that he will not let himself be changed by machines but will himself change the machine; and whatever he looks like he will above all look human.

I would now like to turn briefly to the comedy *Mann ist Mann* [*A Man's a Man*] and explain why this introduction about the new human type was necessary. Of course not all these problems are going to arise and be elucidated in this particular play. They will be elucidated somewhere quite different. But it struck me that all sorts of things in *Mann ist Mann* will probably seem odd to you at first—especially what the central figure, the packer Galy Gay, does or does not do—and if so it's better that you shouldn't think you are listening to an old acquaintance talking about you or himself, but to a new sort of type, possibly an ancestor of just that new human type I spoke of. It may be interesting for you to look straight at him from this point of view, so as to bring out his attitude to things as precisely as possible. You will see that among other things he is a great liar and an incorrigible optimist; he can fit in with anything, almost without difficulty. He seems to be used to putting up with a great deal. It is in fact very seldom that he can allow himself an opinion of his own. For instance when . . . he is offered an utterly spurious elephant which he can resell, he will take care not to voice any opinion of it once he hears a possible purchaser is there. I imagine also that you are used to treating a man as a weakling if he can't say no, but this Galy Gay is by no means a weakling; on the contrary he is the strongest of all. That is to say he becomes the strongest once he has ceased to be a private person; he only becomes strong in the mass. And if the play finishes up with him conquering an entire fortress this is only because in doing so he is apparently carrying out the unqualified wish of a great mass of people who want to get through the narrow pass that the fortress guards. No doubt you will go on to say that it's a pity that a man should be tricked like this and simply forced to surrender his precious ego, all he possesses (as it were); but it isn't. It's a jolly business. For this Galy Gay comes to no harm; he wins. And a man who adopts such an attitude is bound to win. But possibly you will come to quite a different conclusion. To which I am the last person to object.[3]

Obviously, the most important implication of this statement rests in Brecht's dynamic conception of the human condition—that within the nature of man there is the ability to transform his environment, socially and technically. The second implication, and the seat of much Brechtian ambiguity, is that the transformation of man, this dynamic change, is accomplished in a surrender of the identity of the individual to the collective: "he becomes the strongest once he has ceased to be a private person; he only becomes strong in the mass."

In *Baal*, the strong and unique identity of the hero becomes one with the natural forces of his world. In the metaphoric structure of the play, Baal is the rain and the river, the sky and the earth as he is subject to these processes. In both *Baal* and *In the Jungle of the Cities*, the protagonists are forced into the realization that they are subject to the "natural" process of consumption. Within *In the Jungle*, especially, there is the strong sense that the only possibility for human contact is in the consumption of one person by another. Certainly one aspect of that sense of consumption comes to life in Shlink's attempt to assume the identity of Garga and impose upon Garga his own identity as lumber merchant; and that process of identifying himself with another human being is put into play with all the erotic overtones of Genet, as Bentley notes in his introduction to the play.

The problem of identity which provided the tension underneath the surface in Brecht's earlier plays determines the structure of *A Man's a Man*; and the action of the play is the imposition of the character of Jeraiah Jip upon the Irish porter, Galy Gay. It is significant that the society into which Galy Gay is absorbed is a military society, one in which function is more important than identity, in which individual characteristics are lost in a uniformity of appearance and action, and in which the individual will is subject to the order and desire of a superior's restrictive discipline. As a metaphor for *mass*, the army works well. Here identity is of less importance than the papers which give one identity, for—officially—the identification card gives you a place and a rôle, and the individual personality can not do that: " 'Military identity cards must in no way be damaged.' A man can be replaced any time, but nothing is sacred any more unless it's identity cards."

Eric Bentley makes the illuminating criticism that the transition from the earlier plays to A *Man's a Man* primarily represents a movement from tragedy to traditional comedy. However, it is also revealing to consider A *Man's a Man* as a departure from traditional comedy in another crucial aspect. The comic structure usually derives from an action in which a disguise, frequently in an inclusive symbolic sense, is assumed by or imposed upon the central figure; and the resolution depends upon the clarification of the identity of this central figure, most significantly, certainly, in the revelation of the identity of the Shakespearean heroine, a recognition with complex implications.

> The society emerging at the conclusion of comedy represents . . . a kind of moral norm, or pragmatically free society. . . . Thus the movement from *pistis* to *gnosis*, from a society controlled by habit, ritual bondage, arbitrary law and the older characters to a society controlled by youth and pragmatic freedom is fundamentally, as the Greek words suggest, a movement from illusion to reality. Illusion is whatever is fixed or defineable, and reality is best understood as its negation: whatever reality is, it's not *that*. Hence the importance of the theme of creating and dispelling illusion in comedy: the illusions caused by disguise, obsession, hypocrisy, or unknown parentage.[4]

In Brecht's play, of course, the disguise is assumed by the protagonist which then, for all practical purposes, becomes his identity; and the play is resolved, not by a revelation of his true identity as Galy Gay, but, rather, with the projection into the future of his own new identity—an incident against which Brecht plays the frustration and confusion of the real Jeraiah Jip. Of course, within the comic perspective, one could argue well that the real Jeraiah Jip is located with more validity and integrity in the transformed personality of Galy-Jip than in the figure of the identity-less soldier.

Surely traditional comedy assumes that there is a validity and integrity in the concept of identity. To a strong degree the comic action is the successful search for identity, the realization of oneself in a social rôle. Recall the prologue from Hofmannsthal's "Prologue to *Baal*" which I quoted in the first chapter: "The actor is the amoeba among all living things and therefore he is symbolic man. The amoeba, that indeterminate primitive creature, which lets the situation dictate whether it should be animal or plant." [5] As Hofmannsthal's analysis senses, Brecht's first play abrogates a traditional concept of identity, emphasizing as it does the environment as the determining agency in a situation and diminishing the importance of the individual will.

Brecht uses the episode "Inside the Pagoda of the Yellow Monks" to project an equivocal and yet utilitarian concept of identity. Exploiting the captured British soldier, Wang makes the drunk Jeraiah Jip into a god and turns a difficult situation into a profitable one.

> What shall we do with him? He's a soldier, so he won't have any sense. A soldier of the queen, covered with vomited liquor, helpless as a barnyard chick, and so drunk his own mother wouldn't know him! One could make a present of him to the police. But what good is that? When the money's all gone, what good is justice? . . . Pick him up and stuff him in the prayer box! . . . And see that his head sticks out at the top. The best thing we can do is make a god out of him.

In the image of the deluded worshippers, Jip is a deity and has no identity as Jeraiah Jip, British soldier. And, when they face the threat of being apprehended and punished as thieves, the three soldiers, who with Jip have robbed the temple, themselves accept the utility of Wang's logic.

> The man you are looking for is not here. But that you may see that the man who you say is here—and who I do not know to be here—is not your man, permit me to explain it all to you with the aid of a drawing. Allow your unworthy servant to draw four criminals with chalk. (*He draws them on the door of the prayer box.*) One of them has a face, so that one sees who he is, but three of them have no faces. They cannot be recognized. Yet the one with the face has no money, therefore he is no thief. But the ones with the money have no faces, therefore they cannot be recognized. That's how it is as long as they are not together. But when they are together, the three headless men grow faces, and other people's money will be found in their pockets. I would never be able to believe you if you said that a man who might be found here was your man.

The transformation of Jeraiah Jip into a god which inspires the donations of the worshippers prepares us for the complete transformation of Galy Gay into Jeraiah. And the anonymity of blank faces is a better choice for Uriah, Jesse, and Polly than the specific identity which they would hold in guilt. When they choose anonymity for themselves they leave Jeraiah to suffer the consequences of his loss of identity. In order to keep from being apprehended, the three soldiers need to complete their team. To be anonymous they must be four, and the innocent and gullible porter, Galy Gay, is available to be transformed.

Despite the comic optimism present in this claim of the possibility of change, Galy Gay is related to the passive protagonists of Brecht's earlier nihilistic plays. Instead of being the victim, like Baal, of Nature, Galy Gay is the victim of his human environment. The situation calls for him to become Jeraiah Jip, and he does. Uriah outlines that necessity.

URIAH   This porter Galy Gay from Kilkoa must become Jeraiah Jip, our comrade.
    THE THREE look the sleeping GALY GAY over.

POLLY How can we get away with it, Uriah? We have
nothing but Jip's papers.

JESSE They're enough. There's got to be a new Jip. Why
all the fuss about people? *One's as good as none at all.*
It's impossible to speak of less than two hundred at a
time. Each can have an opinion of his own, of course.
What difference does that make? A quiet man can
quietly appropriate two or three opinions-of-his-own.
Men of character? Kiss my ass.

POLLY But what will he say when we turn him into the
soldier Jeraiah Jip?

JESSE A man like that does the turning all on his own.
Throw him into a puddle and he'll grow webs between
his fingers in two days.

The image of Galy Gay as the caricature of this grotesque and comic evolutionary process is fulfilled in the
metamorphosis he experiences. The metaphor is important because it clarifies the action—the transformation is
not a willed progress but rather an adaptation to environment. The difference in *A Man's a Man* comes, certainly,
in the presence of the three soldiers, particularly Uriah
Shelley, as agents, remaking Galy Gay in the image of
Jeraiah Jip—as a conscious and willed action of their own.

While Brecht discusses the change in identity which
takes place in Galy Gay as a "jolly business," an implicit
horror of the collective identity of the army is clear in the
comedy. Willett describes it as "the farce of the military
Team Spirit," [6] and Esslin feels that the comedy grasps
"the essence of later brainwashing techniques." [7] Certainly
Brecht's remarks in the radio speech quoted above assume
the value of the collective in *A Man's a Man*. In that
critical statement the transformation of Galy Gay is seen
as a metaphor for the potential improvement of man
himself. It is important to realize that between the first
performance of *A Man's a Man* and the event of that
radio speech, Brecht began his study of Marxism with a
reading of *Das Kapital*. In his didactic introduction to the
radio performance of the play, Brecht ignores the ambiguous exploration of the conflict between the individual and

the collective which is of such significance in A *Man's a
Man* and which was to provide the substance for much of
his later drama. It is a crucial point in A *Man's a Man*
when Galy Gay in the image of Jeraiah Jip confronts the
coffin which is supposed to contain the body of Galy
Gay—and which does in a symbolic sense. This is the
event of the acceptance of his new identity; and, during a
moment of acute tension, his imagination embraces both
identities before he is able to cut himself apart from the
reflected image of Galy Gay. The pain of this rendering
cannot be ignored.

> *I could not look without dropping dead on the spot*
> *At a face emptied out in a crate*
> *Face of a certain person known to me once*
> *From the shimmering surface of the water into which*
> *Someone looked and then*
> *As I should know*
> *Perished.*
> *And so I cannot open up this crate*
> *Because of this fear that is in both of me.*
> *For perhaps*
> *I am a Both that once*
> *The changing surface of the earth produced*
> *Tied to a navel, formed like a bat, and hanging*
> *Between rubber trees and hut by night,*
> *A Thing that would like to be gay.*
> *One man is no man: someone must call him something.*
> *And so*
> *I would have gladly looked in this trough*
> *Because the heart is tied to the parent's heart, but*
> *If the difference between yes and no is not so great*
> *And if I did not look at the elephant*
> *I close one eye in what concerns myself and shed*
> *What's not acceptable in me and so become*
> *A nice man.*

That moment in which the choice is made to leave the
realized individuality, the familiar image in the reflected
water, is a poignant one. It is a choice between that which
the particular consciousness affirms as identity in a conscious realization of individuality, of being something sep-

arate and unique, and that which is "named," identified by others. In the conclusion of this passage, Gay devalues the existence of the individual in his claim that both identities, the old and the new, are wet by the rain, dried by the wind, and sustained by feeding:

> And I (*the first I and the second*)
> *We inspect the rain and the wind*
> *That wets us and that dries us, and*
> *We build our strength by eating.*

He negates individuality claiming that one man is as good as another, one identity as good as another. Then, asking the questions "can you see me at all? Where am I? . . . What am I doing?" he performs like a soldier and is identified by them as Jeraiah Jip—putting the responsibility for personal identity upon those who name him.

Ronald Gray is sensitive to the puzzling ambiguity of Brecht's attitude towards the collective in *A Man's a Man*. In his discussion of the transformation of Galy Gay, Gray writes

the events are not related entirely in a tone of 'artistic' neutrality. A deliberate interruption is made by one of the characters, who advances to inform the audience of the author's intentions, and thus for the first time an element of 'Verfremdung' or 'estrangement'—a term used later by Brecht in his theoretical writings . . . , whose sense will be seen gradually developing in these earlier works—is clearly introduced. Yet the intentions, for all that, are not made particularly clear. There is some concern, it is true, about the possibility that a character like Galy Gay can be so transformed:

> *They'll soon, if we don't watch over him*
> *In the wink of an eye make a butcher of him.*

The imperialism caricatured in the play is plainly denounced. At the same time, however, a behaviouristic view of human nature is adopted, which is ultimately neutral once again. Whatever a man is made to become, the commentator continues, no mistake will have been made: his human nature is as capable of monstrosities as of what used to be called humanity. . . . In this way the ground is cut away from the moral protest that seemed about to be made, and the play proceeds on a level of ambiguity that has allowed at least two critics, mindful perhaps of Brecht's similarity to Galy Gay, to see even wisdom in the adaptability to circumstance he displays. The continuing adherence to a neutralist or indifferentist view militates against the desire to affirm moral tenets, and the play leaves a bewildering impression of a ferocious irony that still leaves the standpoint of the ironist uncertain.[8]

One thing, surely, which contributes to this equivocation is the fact that Galy Gay assumes the role of Jeraiah Jip through guilt and through fear for his own safety. It is not merely the process of an indeterminate creature realizing an identity through adapting to an environment. In one sense, Galy Gay consciously wills himself into his new self in order to escape from the consequences of being Galy Gay. However, the whole ridiculous episode is structured and played as a comic routine, to convince the gullible Galy Gay of his own guilt so that he will elect the identity of Jeraiah Jip. Significantly, the obviously fictitious elephant becomes real to Galy Gay only when it becomes, apparently, marketable. And during the transaction he is a man "who wants his name kept out of it" for his own protection. Then, when it appears as though the selling of the elephant were illegal, Galy Gay claims that he is not Galy Gay. He denies his real identity in order to be free from the consequences of his crime, and it is ironic that this action, for which he is afraid to suffer the consequences, is no action at all but rather a grotesque and ironic improvisation. This irony is emphasized in the comic logic which says that Galy Gay is guilty of stealing and selling an army elephant and also guilty of the felonious sale of an elephant which did not exist.

> Pay attention, pal, because, firstly, you stole and sold an army elephant, which is larceny, because, secondly, you sold an elephant which was not an elephant, which is fraud, and because, thirdly, you have neither a name nor an identity card and may be a spy or even a swindler who gave the wrong name at roll-call.

In fear of being shot, Galy Gay denies that he is Galy Gay and becomes Jeraiah Jip.

> Oh, not so fast! I'm not the man you are looking for. I don't even know him. My name is Jip, I swear it. What is an elephant compared to a man? And I don't even know the creature. I didn't see the elephant. . . . I'm someone else. At most I bear that man some very slight resemblance, and you confuse me with him. I am not Galy Gay. I am not.

The logic by which Galy Gay denies his own identity is the same as that which Wang uses to convince the stealing trio of soldiers that they are not themselves and that Jeraiah Jip is not himself but, rather, a god. Certainly it is important to realize that all changes of identity which take place in Brecht's comedy occur for two reasons. In the first place, the identity is changed so that one person or persons can exploit another; the change itself is an exploitation. Also, the personal motive within the person who allows the change is a strong fear of the consequences of some action. And, interestingly enough, both Jeraiah Jip and Galy Gay allow the change through their own greed. Gay pretends to recognize the reality of the elephant when he sees the possibility of making money from its sale, and Jip allows himself to be exploited as a god when he is plied with food and drink and realizes the safety of his rôle. Exploitation and greed accomplish the "jolly business" of changing the nature of man; and, in the puzzling ethical structure of the play, the value given this absorption of the individual by the collective is questioned. The loss of individuality which these changes cause is declared to be of little importance because "A man's a man," and one is as good—or as bad—as another because their function and not their unique identity is the important aspect of their humanity.

Approximately the same time as Brecht was working on A Man's a Man, he was clarifying his ideas on the nature and the function of the theatre—its relationship to the audience, the social environment, and the ideological de-

velopments of the time. Brecht's attitude toward the theatre is illustrated by his desire to have the theatrical experience be more analogous to the event in the sporting arena:
a detached, objective, and brilliantly clear demonstration
of technique, with the aesthetic satisfaction coming from
the skill of the game well-played.

> When people in sporting establishments buy their tickets
> they know exactly what is going to take place; and that is
> exactly what does take place once they are in their seats:
> viz. highly trained persons developing their peculiar powers
> in the way most suited to them, with the greatest sense of
> responsibility yet in such a way as to make one feel that
> they are doing it primarily for their own fun. *Against that
> the traditional theatre is nowadays quite lacking in char-
> acter.*[9]

A desire for audiences to be clearly aware of the nature of
their experience in the theatre and for the audience and
actor to enjoy the performance is implicit in this declaration. And, like the sporting event, the fun derives from the
exercising and witnessing of skill. Brecht's implicit desire
for clarity is the most important point of this article: the
spectator should not be confused or ambiguous in his
response to the performance; clarity, not emotion, is the
objective. In Brecht's developing ethic the theatre's falsity
derives from the emotionality of the performance, an emotional intensity which misdirects the spectator's response,
deceiving him into accepting as valid an imitation of
human experience which is untrue.

> Behind a feigned intensity you are offered a naked strug-
> gle in lieu of real competence. They no longer know how
> to stage anything remarkable, and therefore worth seeing.
> In his obscure anxiety not to let the audience get away the
> actor is immediately so steamed up that he makes it seem
> the most natural thing in the world to insult one's father.
> At the same time it can be seen that acting takes a tremen-
> dous lot out of him. *And a man who strains himself on the
> stage is bound, if he is any good, to strain all the people
> sitting in the stalls.*[10]

His public letter to the sociologist, Mr. X., clarifies the motive behind Brecht's demand for clarity. In this statement, Brecht argues against the aesthetic which would claim that the theatre provides a ritual function in the enactment of typical, or archetypal, human actions, offering the spectator primarily an emotional satisfaction. In this article, Brecht defines the function of the theatre as an agency for social change. Brecht had already related the theatre to the sporting event in which the vital exercise of skill and the clarity of the spectator's reaction provide excitement and fun. Here he moves toward his scientific conception of mimesis, the use of the theatre as an arena for the exploration of human behavior in order to determine valid and ethical actions:

> When I invited you [Fritz Sternberg, the sociologist who worked with Brecht in a plan to produce *Julius Caesar* with Piscator] to look at the drama from a sociological point of view I did so because I was hoping that sociology would be the death of our existing drama. As you immediately saw, there was a simple and radical task for sociology: to prove that there was no justification for this drama's continued existence and no future for anything based (now or in the future) on the assumptions which once made drama possible. To quote a sociologist whose vocabulary I hope we both accept, there is no sociological space for it.[11]

Brecht declares the aesthete would claim that drama could be improved but only through the "tricks of the trade," improved structure, and more convincing motivation. The sociologist, in Brecht's imagination, is free to disregard such banal judgments as 'good' and 'bad' or 'beautiful' and concentrate upon the primary aesthetic concern, in Brecht's mind, the correctness or falsity of the work. It is clear that Brecht's radical rejection of the traditional theatre derives from his conception of the theatrical performance as social action; the play, which cannot be divorced from the social nature of the performance, derives from man's social needs, the dynamics of social change. In its intricate relationship to the social situation, the epic theatre should certainly provide emotional satisfaction, but—in Brecht's terms—that emotion would have validity and use. Brecht's concept of the theatre as agency is clear in his use of the Marxist phrase, the "ideological superstructure" as he writes, "it is precisely theatre, art and literature which have to form the 'ideological superstructure' for a solid practical rearrangement of our age's way of life." Brecht continues his discussion of the nature of an *epic theatre*:

> In its works the new school of play-wrighting lays down that the *epic theatre* is the theatrical style of our time. To expound the principles of the epic theatre in a few catch-phrases is not possible. They still mostly need to be worked out in detail, and include representation by the actor, stage technique, dramaturgy, stage music, use of the film, and so on. The essential point of the epic theatre is perhaps that it appeals less to the feelings than to the spectator's reason. Instead of sharing an experience the spectator must come to grips with things. At the same time it would be quite wrong to try and deny emotion to this kind of theatre. It would be much the same thing as trying to deny emotion to modern science.[12]

In this early description of the epic theatre Brecht sees the dramatic act in terms of function, a utilitarian conception of art somewhat analogous to Kenneth Burke's notion of art as strategic act. Of course, Burke's sense of the strategic nature of the artistic act is a psychic process and not necessarily a rational one. While Brecht would deny, consciously and strongly, the validity of a critical exploration of his poetry as the manifestation of his own imagination, it is illuminating to see how his use of the dramatic act as social function is related to its function within his own imagination. Consider Burke's most familiar and, perhaps, crucial critical statement:

> Critical and imaginative works are answers to questions posed by the situation in which they arose. They are not merely answers, they are *strategic* answers, *stylized* answers. . . . I should propose an initial working distinction between 'strategies' and 'situations,' whereby we think of poetry (I here use the term to include any work of critical

or imaginative cast) as the adopting of various strategies for the encompassing of situations. These strategies size up the situations, name their structure and outstanding ingredients, and name them in a way that contains an attitude toward them.[13]

As these discussions of the earlier plays have attempted to clarify, Brecht's works are strategies to encompass his strong compassion, an acute feeling for human suffering which exists in a world in which that suffering cannot be alleviated. It is important to realize that in Brecht's own dramatic process he names the structure of the situation. In *Baal* he names the structure of the cosmos in metaphysical terms. Within *In the Jungle of the Cities*, of course, he defines the absurdity of the cosmos, its irrationality, in terms of the isolation of the human soul, the impossibility of any individual achieving a meaningful relationship with another. The very rehearsal of that isolation demonstrates that, within his own imagination, Brecht valued the possibility of some meaningful human relationship. The plays are testaments of Brecht's own anguish; otherwise there would not be the need to define the absurdity and describe the human suffering that such cosmic absurdity causes. In *Baal* and *In the Jungle of the Cities*, the playwright's acute anguish exists without hope; the works despair in their complete nihilism.

In *Baal*, Brecht seems to concentrate primarily upon Baal and his puzzling, equivocal relationship with Nature. The playwright begins to explore the nature of human relationships in his description of the destructive encounters of men and women with Baal who sees them, and uses them, merely as objects to be consumed and discarded. With *In the Jungle of the Cities*, Brecht focuses upon the organized level of social existence. The grotesque Chicago of the play—the complex product of civilization—becomes the image of absurdity, replacing the natural world of *Baal* with its man-made equivalent. In *A Man's a Man*, the relationship between agent and victim, which in *Baal* is the conflict between Nature and will, is the tension between the individual and the collective. The qualities of

Nature, represented in the energy of the onrushing river, become the qualities of the army, the collective, the group, the mass. Galy Gay is subject to the collective in a sense analogous to Baal's acceptance of the tyranny of Nature. And the ambiguity which is contained in the Nature of Brecht's first play is displaced in the complexity of his image of the collective in *A Man's a Man*.

In his discussion of the relationship between Marx and Sartre, Norman N. Greene makes the following observation about the difference in their concept of Nature; and it is useful to clarify Brecht's relationship to this dichotomy.

It should be noted here that materialism is possible as a revolutionary doctrine because of a basic assumption which Sartre does not share; namely the beneficence of the natural order. This is evident above all in the important role which the dialectic holds in the Marxist system; it is basically a version of natural law which retains its descriptive and normative functions. Sartre's view of nature has already been discussed; it is present at the heart of his philosophy, in the distinction which he makes between being-in-itself and being-for-itself. Being-in-itself, which corresponds to nature, has the being of objective fact, whereas being-for-itself, or human consciousness, is the source of all values. Marxist dialectical materialism betrays a nonreflective optimism about the relations between man and the natural order which may be a requirement of the revolutionary attitude. Sartre, who holds out his philosophy as a superior alternative to Marxism, nowhere explicitly traces materialism to this origin. Nevertheless, this point is implicit in all his criticisms of Marxism as a social doctrine.[14]

It is quite clear that Brecht shares a sense of man alienated from a chaotic and meaningless Nature with the existentialists; and yet, as I hope the discussion of *Baal* demonstrates, Brecht's attitude toward Nature is a complex one, an erotic fascination and fear—a fear which comes most strongly, of course, when Brecht senses that the irrationality of Nature determines man's fate through the irrationality of his own human nature. After these early plays, in which Nature plays such a dominant role, Brecht focuses upon man in relationship with man, and Nature in the earlier sense is present only in the demand to have the action occur somewhere. Nature is environment only in a most general sense. Civilization, not Nature, provides the determining environment. To a degree, Brecht blocks out Nature in the sense that it exists in *Baal* and some of the earlier poems until it again becomes an active force in *The Caucasian Chalk Circle*. Perhaps this abandonment of Nature as poetic environment takes place because Brecht's concerns are less metaphysical in the plays after *In the Jungle of the Cities*. The thematic concerns remain the same, but these cares are more specifically explored in man's relationship with man; and the extension of the human consciousness into its metaphysical relationship with the cosmos is subordinate to the dialectic of man's conflict with man which assumes, in Marxist terms a "natural" improvement. Brecht's discovery of Marxism with its optimism, its sense of dynamic social change, gave him a specific channel into which to direct the energy of his compassion. However, the more essential tension, the conflict between the individual will and that which restricts it, remains for him to consider. For this reason, the collective, the mass, can never exist in his poetry as pure value. As the next chapter discusses, this ambiguity of attitude toward the collective exists strongly even in Brecht's clearest and most explicitly polemic play, *The Measures Taken*.

In *A Man's a Man*, Nature is still present, particularly in the debilitating sexuality of "Bloody Five," Charles Fairchild. The obvious point of reference between *Baal* and *A Man's a Man* is the analogy between Sergeant Fairchild's submission to sensuality during rainy weather and Baal's own sense of sexual instinct as an aspect of Nature. The concept of man's vulnerability to the forces of Nature, carried in the images of the river, storms, and the sky itself which are so lyrically used in *Baal*, becomes the grotesque and bawdy joke about the sexuality of "Bloody Five."

It's well known in army circles that in time of rainfall he succumbs to terrible attacks of sensuality. He's completely changed, inside and out. . . . It need only start raining, and Bloody Five, the most dangerous man in the Indian Army, is as undangerous as a milk-tooth, for, when it rains, Bloody Five is transformed into The Bloody Gent, and The Bloody Gent concentrates on girls for three days on end.

Charles Fairchild, "Bloody Five," who takes great pride in his identity as the fierce sergeant, sees man's loss of control in sexual behavior as something evil. He shouts at Widow Begbick: "I tell you I'd like to see the whole thing go up in flames, this Sodom of the rocking-chair and whiskey bar, and you with it, for you're a Gomorrah in yourself, you gobble me up when you look at me like that, you white-washed Babylon. . . . The human race began to disintegrate when the first muttonhead failed to button up."

"Bloody Five" finds his identity, his manliness, in his military rôle. He sees his identity destroyed in the sexual act, an experience in which he is consumed; because in surrendering to passion, he becomes weak and passive, no longer the strong and commanding Sergeant "Bloody Five." However, in an interesting paradox, "Bloody Five" does not see his identity lost in the army, but, rather he conceives of the army as a means of gaining identity. He says: "As a book, the army field manual has its shortcomings, but it's the only one a man can depend on, if he *is* a man, because it gives him a backbone, and accepts full responsibility before God." In this strange comedy Fairchild castrates himself in order to gain control over the instinct which threatens to destroy his reputation as "Bloody Five." It is significant that, in Brecht's imagination, the name becomes of such importance. After Jesse and Uriah have "shanghaied" Galy Gay on the train for battle and have begun to convince him that he is indeed Jeraiah Jip, Polly worries that he will read his name in his papers and "go right off his head." Jesse comments on the value of identity cards since even the best of men, the best of soldiers, have faulty memories. He concludes: "One's name! If a man were to think of his name too often, that wouldn't be good." Immediately after this comment, we hear the voice of Fairchild crying:

> What shame has come over me? Where is my name that was a byword from Calcutta to Cooch Behar? Where is the yesterday that is gone forever. . . . It is not important that I eat: it is important that I am Bloody Five. It's as simple as that. . . . Here's a rope. Here's an army pistol. What do you know? Rebels are always shot. It's as simple as that! 'Pack your bag now, Johnny!' No girl in the world will ever cost me a penny again! That's it. It's as simple as that. I needn't even take my pipe out of my mouth. I hereby assume my responsibilities. I must do it—to remain Bloody Five. Fire!

This act of castration, the assertion of Fairchild's own will, is one of those rare instances in Brechtian drama, in which a character does assert himself, attempting to gain a control over the instinct to which he is subject. In general, Brecht's characters are not agents; rather they are patients who surrender to irrational actions imposed upon them by Nature, social conditions, or the irrational events of the moment. Herbert Lindenberger makes this point in his brief comparison of Brecht and Büchner.

> Like Büchner, Brecht has a penchant for passive heroes who allow the world to shape them as it will; Brecht, indeed, has perhaps gone further than any major dramatist in exploring the psychology of passivity—for instance, in the well-meaning porter Galy Gay in *Man Equals Man* (1926), who is cajoled into assuming the identity of another man and becoming a brutal soldier.[15]

Baal is passive, in a special sense of submitting to an energy which is not part of his own conscious mind; Shlink and Garga suffer without being able to will a positive action; Galy Gay assumes the quality of another identity which is given him and his extraordinary vitality as a soldier comes from his passive acceptance of the rôle. "Bloody Five" is the exception; he has suffered the influence of the rain and the debilitating of his military strength, and rather than continue to surrender himself to sexual instinct, he asserts himself in the act of self-castration. This destruction of his sexual identity is but an affirmation of his control of experience. In a sense, this action is the single existential assertion in the early Brecht. Fairchild's act of assertion is a sacrifice of masculinity made to maintain his identity in the minds of others. Galy Gay, who has learned just how insignificant a name can be, sees this action as foolish:

> On account of his name, this gentleman did something very bloody to himself. He shot his sex away. I was very fortunate to see it, for now I see where pigheadedness leads, and what a bloody thing it is for a man to be dissatisfied with himself and make such a fuss about his name!

Yet, in a basic sense, this act of the will is an acceptance of the collective as much as Galy Gay's passive acceptance of an imposed identity. "Bloody Five's" refusal to be the victim of natural sexuality is his surrender to the collective in which he can now function efficiently without the noisome interruptions caused by the demands of his sexuality.

In a discussion of the relationship of the early Brecht to the later existentialists, it is important to consider the passivity of Brecht's early heroes; the nature of the action of acceptance. This hero does not gain his identity in his choice but rather in the identification of himself with the irrational forces of Nature. In the sense of the absurdity of the universe, the Brechtian despair is an existential anguish, but Brecht's conception of human action in the early plays is not existential. In existential terms, the irrationality, the absurdity, of the universe provides an ultimate freedom: the consequence of alienation is freedom. Act itself is the choice of oneself; and the human determines his reality in his choice:

> Human reality can not receive its ends, as we have seen, either from outside or from a so-called inner 'nature.' It chooses them and by this very choice confers upon them a transcendent existence as the external limit of its projects.

From this point of view—and if it is understood that the existence of the *Dasein* precedes and commands its essence—human reality in and through its very upsurge decides to define its own being by its ends. It is therefore the positing of my ultimate ends which characterizes my being and which is identical with the sudden thrust of the freedom which is mine.[16]

In Charles Fairchild's self-castration in A *Man's a Man,* Brecht only seems to affirm the possibility of a human being free to make a choice which will work toward the determination of his own identity. Fairchild realizes his identity as the ferocious "Bloody Five" when he "plucks out" that offensive sexuality which makes him subject to his own instincts—instincts which are stimulated by rain, identifying sexual instinct with Brecht's concept of Nature as agent. This grotesque act of human freedom, of course, parallels the change in identity which occurs in Galy Gay. However, Gay is the passive victim of this change. He does not choose but, like the passive hero of *Baal* and *In the Jungle of the Cities,* he accepts that which is determined outside of his own consciousness, becoming what is necessary for him to become.

A *Man's a Man* is a puzzling and equivocal play as all works are which are generated in a transitional phase in the artist's own conception of reality. And, ironically, it lacks the very clarity which Brecht's theoretical writings demand. Marxism provided Brecht with a means to use the compassion which is so strong in his early work. Marx's humanism assumes that while the universe cannot be teleological in any metaphysical sense, that in mankind, as an agency, there is the possibility of change: in the synthesis there can be a progress. Any consideration of Brecht's Marxism must respond to this celebration of human possibility. But this celebration is complicated by Brecht's equivocal conception of the collective. In A *Man's a Man,* he is moving toward a concept of the collective which reaches its strongest statement in *The Measures Taken.* The action in A *Man's a Man* is the movement from a realized individuality toward an identity derived from the function within an organization—from self-realization to social function. The irony in Brecht comes as the collective, which is society, becomes the devouring beast, the destructive force to which the hero is subject. That concept is informed in complex ways with the ever-present conflict between will and passivity. In *A Man's a Man* the result is an equivocal, although entertaining, play. In *The Measures Taken, Galileo,* and *Mother Courage,* the conflict resounds in a tragic paradox. As the more detailed discussions of these plays will show, Brecht never resolved this conflict between the individual and the collective in his own imagination. Throughout his work, Brecht celebrates the vitality of the individual at the same time he explicitly projects the ethic of the collective.

4

The Measures Taken: Instinctive Compassion and the Collective Ethic

In its probing of the relationship between the individual and the collective, *A Man's a Man* anticipates the subject which Brecht explores in his dramatizations of the Marxist polemic. Brecht turned to the study of *Das Kapital* immediately after he finished his work on *A Man's a Man*,[1] and from this point on, Brecht's dramaturgy functioned consciously in terms of the Marxist dialectic. Of course, Brecht's next major work was his collaboration with Kurt Weill in the amazingly successful *The Threepenny Opera*, a work which continues the fragmented perspectives of *A Man's a Man*. This earthy and vigorous musical comedy presents a picture of mankind in what is intended to be a devastating satire of capitalism in an equation of property and theft. However, the focus of the satire is diffused in a complex of ironies. In an environment as exploitative as the society of *The Threepenny Opera*, Macheath's crimes do not assume the quality of abstract bourgeois evil; and his vitality gives him a certain charm which dulls the edge of the satire. Despite the aesthetic distancing which both the satire and the epic staging accomplish, the poet's compassion for these figures who are subjected to the exploitative dealings of this world is clear. The concluding lines seem to revert to the stark nihilism of the earlier Brecht:

> *Remember: this whole vale of tribulation*
> *Is black as pitch and cold as any stone.*

The positive materialism of the philosophy of Karl Marx provided Bertolt Brecht with a means of alleviating the despair of his nihilism. In the earlier chapters I defined the nature of that nihilism and discussed the plays as manifestations of Brecht's existential despair in which the universe seems to be an irrational chaos with no teleological agency. Brecht seems to suffer from this sense of cosmic irrationality most acutely as it limits individual freedom, circumscribing the action of the particular will which can do nothing but submit to the arbitrary energies it encounters. In this vision of the human condition Brecht saw man controlled in his relationships with other men by the operation of some natural law of consumption. The Marxist outcry against the mass exploitation of human beings appealed to Brecht and gave him a method of implementing his compassion in the specific act of playwriting.

Brecht's need to use the poetic act as a social instrument is seen in the anguish of "Concerning The Infanticide, Marie Farrar." The ambiguous assignment of guilt in this early poem contains an implicit demand for social reform even though the nature of that reform is unclear. All of Brecht's early work contains a strong sense of compassion, but nowhere is its appeal as explicit as in this poem. Here Brecht tells the story of a young servant girl who gives birth to an illegitimate child and then destroys it. In this grotesque ballad he presents an event which is, probably, the most despicable crime imaginable—an infanticide. Brecht presents the crime in clearly lighted details.

> *The child began to cry until*
> *It drove her mad so that she says*
> *She did not cease to beat it with her fists*
> *Blindly for some time till it was still.*
> *And then she took the body to her bed*
> *And kept it with her there all through the night.*[2]

Yet Brecht's presentation of her hysteria, her painful suffering, the silence which answers her innocent prayers, her patient submission to the demands of her unseeing employers, and the agony of the birth itself in the snow-filled latrine—all work to mitigate her crime, and the reader is asked to respond to the recurrent call for pity:

> *But you, I beg you, check your wrath and scorn,*
> *For man needs help from every creature born.*

There is no divine impulse present here to reconcile injustice, and no Christian heaven to exist as a reward for human suffering. Consequently the burden of guilt for injustice and misery is mankind's own. Our compassion for the criminal Marie Farrar is necessary because we, who allow such meaningless deprivation and pain, are equally guilty: "So let it be a judgment upon both you and me." The poem itself ends:

> *Marie Farrar, born in April,*
> *An unmarried mother, convicted, died in*
> *The Meissen penitentiary,*
> *She brings home to you all men's sin.*
> *You who bear pleasantly between clean sheets*
> *And give the name 'blessed' to your womb's weight*
> *Must not damn the weakness of the outcast,*
> *For her sin was black but her pain was great.*

In the nihilism of the early plays, there does not seem to be the possibility of an ethic which would admit that one individual is responsible for his exploitation of another. The responsibility for that exploitation is in the natural law which is fulfilled in such exploitation. "Concerning The Infanticide, Marie Farrar," however, anticipates Brecht's sense of an ethical commitment to the collective in the poet's acceptance of the responsibility for the servant girl's act. The acceptance of guilt in this poem provides a significant moment in Brecht's poetry. If the poet and his audience are responsible for the sordid deprivation which makes such an act inevitable, then there must be an alternative behavior within their will. If there were no alternative behavior, neither the poet nor his audience would be burdened with the guilt which cries out so strongly in this poem. The alternative, of course, came to Brecht in the form of Marxist humanism—in an idealistic vision of a world in which creative human relationships are a possibility. In the nihilistic world vision of the early Brecht, human energy is seen as an impetus to consume, an impulse which is part of a natural destruction. Marx's sense of human passion as the energy of the individual moving towards its object includes a sense of human love as the communion of one person with another.

> Let us assume *man* to be *man*, and his relation to the world to be a human one. Then love can only be exchanged for love, trust for trust, etc. . . . If you wish to influence other people you must be a person who really has a stimulating and encouraging effect upon others. Every one of your relations to man and to nature must be a *specific expression*, corresponding to the object of your will, of your *real individual* life. If you love without evoking love in return, i.e., if you are not able, by the *manifestation* of yourself as a loving person, to make yourself a *beloved person*, then your love is impotent and a misfortune.[3]

Here is a sense of a social structure built upon compassion, understanding, and trust. However, what is most significant in this passage from *Economic and Philosophical Manuscripts* is the sense that the humanity of man derives from his ability to love and to be loved—in the identification of the will with another being in unique and specific encounters.

Brecht's conversion to Marxism is marked by a radical transformation of the nature of his plays. The concepts of the epic theatre which were under experimentation, particularly in *A Man's a Man*, developed into a clear formalism in the teaching plays, the *Lehrstuecke*, of the early 1930's. The abstract quality of these plays is achieved in their simplicity, their rational use of conventions to project an idea with precision and clarity. While Brecht's gradual movement toward his "epic" means of imitating reality began before his definite commitment to Communism, his forming aesthetic certainly worked to serve the Marxist intent of his plays, especially the *Lehrstuecke*. The most important aspect of Brecht's new aesthetic is its relationship to objective reality.

The question of realism in the theatre is, perhaps, the most difficult problem in aesthetics which the playwright, actor, producer, and critic faces. The naturalist claims realism in his representation which is as direct as imitation of the external qualities of nature as the basic convention of the theatre allows. The symbolist claims that his presentation projects a sense of 'inner reality.' The Epic Theatre of Bertolt Brecht accepts the reality of the external world and claims the stage as a platform upon which some experience from the external world is demonstrated. While each theatrical form is based upon illusion, the playwright manipulates the spectator's sense of reality, focusing it upon the symbol and its evocations, or upon the moral problems demonstrated upon the stage.[4]

Like the theatricalism of Pirandello, Brecht's distancing of dramatic action uses the obvious artifice of the dramatic event to serve the playwright in his attempt to clarify some aspect of human experience. But, where Pirandello's fragmentations of experience deny the validity of locating reality in any specific place—that is, the consciousness of the spectator, the imagination of the playwright, or the external, objective world—Brecht's sense of the epic theatre assumes the validity of an objective world and the possibility of man relating to it. The epic theatre assumes that in this objective world certain injustices occur, and—in the arena of the theatre, these injustices and their alternative modes of behavior can be *demonstrated*, enacted in a certain objectivity so that the rational mind of the spectator is free to make an ethical judgment. As early as 1926, Brecht wrote

I cannot agree with those who complain of no longer being in a position to prevent the imminent decline of the west. I believe that there is such a wealth of subjects . . . worth learning that once a good sporting spirit sets in one would have to build theatres if they did not already exist. The most hopeful element, however, in the present-day theatre is the people who pour out of both ends of the building after the performance. They are dissatisfied.[5]

Brecht objected to the emotional aspect of *mimesis* as Aristotle's *Poetics* defines it. Brecht saw the function of the theatre as a rational clarification rather than an emotional purging. He considered the manipulation of emotion to be immoral and futile. The emotional exploitation of the spectator's imagination, in which his rational sense is deadened in his empathic identification with the characters, appalled Brecht; and he demanded a form in which such identification would be controlled or at least diminished. The primary aspect of this new form is seen in his sense of dramatic structure. Action in the Aristotelian concept of unity is seen as the imitating of a crucial moment in a complex development—a unified progress through an acutely felt experience in which there is a transition in the protagonist as he responds, progressively, to the nature of the experience. In Brecht, the event is presented from a variety of perspectives in a series of episodes, which are related—but more through the thematic structure than in the organization of the progressive steps of a specific human experience. It was Brecht's intention that this episodic structure would abrogate the possibility of the spectator responding to the action as a psychic experience in which his imagination would identify with that of the hero. The rest of the features of the epic theatre are extensions of this concept of the emotional alienation or detachment, the *Verfremdungseffekt*: the signs and projections which describe the nature of the individual scenes, the half-curtain which does not fully cover the scene changes, the exposed spotlights, the use of masks and makeup which are obviously unreal. Brecht intended that all these devices would work to keep the spectator in rational control of his emotions so that the stage could become a space for social experimentation. It is important to realize that Brecht saw the theatre as an important social activity, responding to a society which he saw as far more complex than that explored in classical or recent serious drama.

> Petroleum resists the five-act form; today's catastrophes do not progress in a straight line but in cyclical crises; the 'heroes' change with the different phases, are interchangeable, etc; the graph of people's actions is complicated by abortive actions; fate is no longer a single coherent power; rather there are fields of force which can be seen radiating

in opposite directions; the power groups themselves comprise movements not only against one another but within themselves. . . . Even to dramatize a simple newspaper report one needs something much more than the dramatic technique of a Hebbel or an Ibsen.

. . . All this, i.e. all these problems, only bears on serious attempts to write *major* plays: something that is at present very far from being properly distinguished from common or garden entertainment. . . . Once we have begun to find our way about the subject-matter we can move on to the relationships, which at present are immensely complicated and can only be simplified by *formal* means. The form in question can however only be achieved by a complete change of the theatre's purpose. Only a new purpose can lead to a new art. The new purpose is called paedagogics.[6]

While Martin Esslin firmly recognizes the naïve fallacies of Brecht's Communism, he sees the aesthetic value which Brecht's polemics wrought:

Brecht's commitment to Marxism . . . gave his anarchic and nihilistic tendencies a rigid framework of intellectual discipline. The inner tension created by this discipline, by the effort to repress the amorphous forces of his subconscious mind, gave Brecht's work its own peculiar spell, its tautness, poetic ambiguity, and depth.[7]

Concentration upon the development of a formal drama with deliberate conventions of its own provided a restraint for Brecht, controlling his energies which had been, to a strong degree, diffused in the earlier plays and using them in a specific act which would accomplish something—which could, the playwright hoped, change mankind if successfully realized.

After the popular success of *The Threepenny Opera,* Brecht and Weill turned to the strict formal control of didactic musical drama. Impelled by the desire to make the aesthetic act a functional one, Brecht saw the epic theatre in its ultimate form with the change in social attitude coming from direct participation in the piece itself. The results of this exploration were the *Lehrstuecke,* short musical dramas written for school children. Within the strict formalism of this work, there is an obvious richness and vitality. Two aspects of these plays are predominant: the strict formal control and the recurrent thematic concern with the denial of the individual feeling to the collective ethic.

It seems quite obvious that the compassion which exists in such a poem as "Concerning the Infanticide, Marie Farrar" is the acutely experienced human feeling which is invested in the collective ideal of *The Measures Taken*. And yet the specific human feeling which causes us to decry the exploitation and deprivation suffered by the individual, Marie Farrar, is projected in the *Lehrstuecke* as futile or destructive, because it does not serve the Communist Party's cause. In this play, individual vitality is destructive; the individual implements his compassion only by becoming an anonymous member of the collective and submitting his human will to the defined ethic of the collective. The sense of compassion which cries out in this play is viewed as human weakness; and, on one level, the action in *The Measures Taken* is the purging of that very weakness.

While *Baal* and *In the Jungle* stand as violent affirmations of vital individualism and celebrate the pure energy of being despite its grotesqueness and absurdity, *The Measures Taken* attempts to deny human feeling and celebrate the loss of identity in the subordination of the individual personality to the abstract ideal. Here the force of instinct can not be entirely dammed up, but its energies can be directed to an ethical objective. Brecht gained a respect for the control of instinct from his reading in Behaviorism, from its faith that man could be directed by rationally generated principles rather than spontaneous emotion. From his study of Communism Brecht gained the promise of control over social cruelty, inequality, and political irrationality. Behaviorism and Communism gave the poet a means of accommodating his nihilistic vision. The ideal of Brecht's polemic provided him with a rational order which he could impose upon the irrational chaos of the human condition. The altruism of Communism made it possible for Brecht, a poet whose work explores and defines the suffering human will, to live with the world as he saw it—"the excrement" of a God who does not exist and whose values do not obtain in human experience which is the only reality. H. R. Hays writes

> there are many poems which deal with decay and death from an ambivalent attitude, a shifting from the philosophy of enjoy-the-moment to a toying with self-annihilation. The symbol of drowning appears again and again joined with an almost pleasurable interest in the gruesome. Whether this indicates a sensitivity to an underlaying death wish in society or traditional German morbidity, it is clear that physical realism prepares us for another attitude which dominates all of the poet's later work. For if the contemplation of misery, physical suffering, and death does not lead to mysticism or evasion, the natural alternative is a scrutiny of the causes for the horrors of existence: a writer who is essentially a materialist will seek for a materialist explanation. And in addition there was always in Brecht enough of the Protestant moralist and prophet to lead him back to the problem of human suffering.[8]

Hays does not relate the "enjoyment-of-the-moment" celebration of human vitality to the pervasive decay so recurrently put forward in the image of the river. This study makes that relationship in an analysis of Brecht's work as the exploration of the human will as it is circumscribed and restricted with external powers. Hays, then, finds Brecht's later work a return to the problem of human suffering. In a larger sense, all of Brecht's work concerns human suffering, as the vitality of the human will is sapped by its conflict with other energies. In the early plays, submission to the external power is seen as a negative action. Baal is the victim of his own instinctive energy, but while his vitality is attractive, his exploitation and consumption of other human beings is not seen as good, in any ethical sense. In the *Lehrstuecke*, the external agent is seen, explicitly, as good. *Einversta endis*, consent, is projected as the ideal action since the discipline to which the hero submits is an absolute value. In these plays of consent the destruction of individuality is extended to the complete sacrifice. The airmen of the *Didactic Play of Baden: On Consent* are willing to die for technological progress; the young child of *He Who Says Yes*, Brecht's adaptation of Arthur Waley's translation of the No play, *Taniko*, consents to the sacrifice demanded by custom; and The Young Comrade of *The Measures Taken*, a play which amplifies the action of the Japanese drama, willingly submits to his death as a necessary step in the progress of the revolution.

In *The Measures Taken*, we find the typical action of the vital human will in a futile struggle with some power or powers imposed upon it in which the will eventually consents to accept that energy and let it take control of him. However, the power which is opposed to the will is assigned to another agent and given a different ethical value. The exercise of compassion in specific acts is seen as a surrender to instinct; and this indulgent submission to the gratification of the emotions is assigned the function which, in the earlier plays, was given to instinctive sexuality. However, while these plays contain a sense of the will's surrender to instinct, they also contain a strong willed consent—a submission to the ethic of the collective which, although valued in the explicit ethical structure of the play, is seen in the typical Brechtian configuration as destructive and self-consuming. In other words, in the power structure which Brecht provides in these plays, the control of instinctive energy is possible in the submission to the collective ethic. However, that submission is a desperate course of action—the destruction of the individual identity, the merging of the individual will with the collective. Here, certainly, is the seat of the tragic paradox which gives *The Measures Taken* such poetic vitality and profundity. But, it is important to remember that, in terms of the ethical structure of the play, Brecht makes it explicitly clear that this action, the submission of the individual to the anonymity of the collective, is good.

The Young Comrade is the vessel for the tension which

provides the tragedy: the conflict maintained between the abstract ideal, which justifies any means, and the specific presence of human feeling, which demands immediate satisfaction. The tragic dilemma exists in the fact that the abstract ideal itself to which human feeling must be sacrificed—the Marxist utopia toward which the agitators are striving—is generated out of human feeling itself. The compassion of The Young Comrade is, symbolically, the source of the ideal of Communism; but that very compassion interferes with the ruthless progress toward the achievement of the ideal. Under the logic which the Party evolves as a means to control suffering, that human feeling must be eliminated. For Ronald Gray, the inadequacy of the social process which Brecht saw as rational destroys the validity of the play.

> The need to come to terms with a social reality as harsh and chaotic as any Germany has seen drove Brecht into a falsity that shows itself in the hysteria of his St Joan and the engineered inhumanity of *The Measures Taken*. Emerging from isolation with a desperate urge to put right the social evils he saw, he fell into the trap that waits for all of us who have a moral conscience: he lost his integrity and became a fanatic.[9]

In *The Measures Taken*, the Marxist doctrine exploits the very pain and deprivation which it seeks to alleviate in order to move the sufferers to revolution; and when The Young Comrade accepts the mission, he submits himself to the logic of the denial of human feeling; his mission is to instruct, agitate, and incite—not to comfort.

> We bring the Chinese workers the teachings of the classics and the propagandists, the ABC of Communism; to the ignorant, instruction about their condition; to the oppressed, class consciousness; and to the class conscious, the experience of revolution.[10]

In order to generate an awareness of the necessity of revolution, comfort must be held in abeyance. The immediate relief which The Young Comrade seeks through tractors, seed, and even munitions is denied.

When The Young Comrade accepts the logic of the suspension of compassion as a rational step in the progress of the revolution, he commits himself to the logic which will, eventually, allow the four agitators to reject their own compassionate response to his suffering and kill him. The Young Comrade cannot control his own sympathies and must accept the necessity of consenting to the only means of controlling his instinctive compassion—his own extinction.

The objective of the first mission assigned to The Young Comrade is to incite the coolies who drag the rice barges up the river from Mukden to demand shoes with wooden soles, in order to establish the strength of the coolies as a force of labor. He is warned: "don't give way to pity!" Immediately, however, the hero experiences the conflict between his commitment to the abstract ideal and a compassion generated by the sight of the coolies in pain and hunger as they pull the barge, chanting their song. When a Coolie falls twice, The Young Comrade cannot resist surrendering to pity, and he cries to the Overseer: "Are you human? I'm going to take a stone and place it here in the mud." Within the rational scheme of the agitators, The Young Comrade's action is foolish on two bases. First of all, the size of his action is ridiculously small in relation to the scope of the problem. The overseer affirms The Young Comrade's folly: "Shoes in Tientsin don't help. I'd rather let our compassionate colleague run ahead with a stone and shove it in front of any worker that slips!" In the second place, his conspicuous action draws attention to his revolutionary behavior so that he and his fellow agitators are pursued and their work delayed.

In his next mission, his sense of justice does not allow him to remain silent when a nonstriking worker is arrested for passing the revolutionary leaflets which he himself is distributing. His interference in the arrest causes the killing of an innocent man; and he, in turn, kills the Policeman. Consequently, the distribution of secret literature is stopped, the police force amplified, and the strikebreaking continued. The Young Comrade is unable to bear the minor injustice of the arrest of the nonstriking worker, and this human weakness results in two killings and the larger injustice, the continuance of the strikebreaking.

The Young Comrade's sense of individuality, manifested in his keen awareness of human feeling, does not allow him to compromise his integrity in social intercourse with The Trader, a man who is useful to the Party because he has considered arming the coolies against their common enemy, the British. The Trader sings "The Song of Merchandise," a ballad of his own exploitation of the coolies, which ends

> Do I know what a man is?
> God knows what a man is!
> I don't know what a man is
> I only know his price.

The Young Comrade conceives of himself as an honest man, not as an agent in the process of revolution; and he refuses to eat with The Trader to conclude the bargaining for weapons. His own sense of his identity as an honest man makes him unable to compromise his integrity for a larger purpose. Again, his indulgence in emotion causes his failure. Here The Control Chorus projects the ethical rationale against which The Young Comrade's behavior seems naïve and egoistic.

> With whom would the right-minded man not sit
> To help the right?
> What medicine would taste too bad
> To a dying man?
> What baseness would you not commit
> To root out baseness?
> If, finally, you could change the world
> What task would you be too good for?
> Who are you?

The value and identity of the individual man is questioned by the action of this little episode. The scene itself is introduced with the query, "What is a Human Being Actually?" The Trader knows the value of a human being in monetary terms, but not his identity. The "Discussion" following the scene calls into question The Young Comrade's own sense of identity and integrity. In a sense there is an analogy between The Trader's conception of man as commodity, an object to be bought and used, and the revolution's use of The Young Comrade as an instrument in the process of social change. Of course, the ultimate foolishness and impetuousity of his idealism is egoistic and selfish in relation to the larger purpose of his mission, but, in this consideration of identity, it is important to respond to the dilemma present in The Young Comrade's imagination who cannot divorce his own concept of himself as a good man from his commitment to the process of achieving good. And Brecht seems to have sensed, although not explicitly, that the revolution's exploitation of The Young Comrade is something akin to The Trader's exploitation of the coolies.

In the final episode of this demonstration of The Young Comrade's failure, his inability to maintain the abstract ideal and resist the temptation to give immediate comfort allows him to support the irrational revolutionary action of the unemployed. The conflict within The Young Comrade between his individual ego and the collective identity of The Party destroys his imagination. The Young Comrade can only accept action which is comprehensible within his own range of vision. He cannot understand the greater perception and wisdom of The Party. The other agitators remind him: "A single man has two eyes. / The Party has a thousand eyes." But the young hero's instinctive response to misery demands its immediate relief; and, most significantly, he senses that their misery cries out to him and that he, specifically, holds the responsibility to correct the situation. There is an interesting parallel here between the action of The Young Comrade in *The Measures Taken* and Shakespeare's conception of sin and guilt in the histories. In *Richard II*, Bolingbroke senses that the revenge for the murder of Gloucester, his uncle, is his responsibility, "which blood, like sacrificing Abel's, cries out, even from the tongueless caverns of the earth to *me*, for justice and rough chastisement." However, despite Bolingbroke's sense of moral agency, in the ethical scheme of Shakespeare's play, the action of justice is the responsibility of the Christian God. Implicit in the ethic of Shakespeare's tetralogy is Bolingbroke's transformation from the naïve consideration of himself as an agent of self-determined justice to the experienced realization that in avenging Richard's crime with Richard's own murder, he himself is also guilty of sin. Completing the poetic integrity of *Richard II*, Bolingbroke equates this sin, as well, to Cain's murder of Abel. In *The Measures Taken*, God as the minister of Justice is replaced by a divine surrogate, the absolute doctrine of the Communist classics. But like the impetuous Bolingbroke, The Young Comrade cannot accept a patient faith in a slow-moving abstract justice and sees himself as judge and magistrate:

> The classics are dirt. I tear them up. For mankind cries out. Its misery tears down the dikes of mere teaching. And that's why I'm for action—right now, this minute! For *I* cry out too. *I* tear down the dikes of mere teaching! . . . I see with my own eyes that misery cannot wait!

Rejecting absolute doctrine, The Young Comrade considers himself to be the focal point of justice:

> Looking at the struggle as it is now, I throw away all that was good yesterday, and do what alone is human. Here is action. I place myself at the head of it. My heart beats for the revolution, and the revolution is here.

He rejects the anonymity he has assumed as an agitator and resumes his own unique identity, acting in opposition to the logic he has accepted:

> *I shall therefore go before them*
> *As what I am*
> *And state*
> *What is.*

The dramatic strength of *The Measures Taken* rests within the integrity of structure and meaning. The little play enacts the subordination of human feeling and hence, human identity, to the abstract ideal; and that subordination is projected in the actual form of the play itself. The action of the play is the sacrifice of the hero, but the poet attempts to destroy the identity of the hero by withdrawing him from the cast of characters present. Baal, Shlink, and Garga are violent affirmations of self-realization; in each of these plays, the primary reality is the self-consciousness of the protagonist. In *The Measures Taken*, Brecht removes the actual presence of the hero and The Young Comrade exists only in his representation by The Four Agitators. The structure of this play deliberately avoids individualization by building the play as a formal demonstration in which The Four Agitators act out, in brief episodes, the sacrifice of The Young Comrade, and the events which make that sacrifice necessary. The characterization of the hero exists only in the demonstrations of the party workers as they share the function of showing his behavior. Yet here Brecht's poetic strength undermines his didactic intention. In spite of his attempt to disintegrate the presence of the hero, the image of The Young Comrade is made vital and real as each agitator illumines another aspect of his behavior and personality. In *The Measures Taken*, as in the classic tragedy, characterization remains abstract but consummately dynamic.

On a symbolic level, the sense of unique and integrated human identity is destroyed as the agitators enact the obliteration of their own individual personalities. At the beginning of their work, the leader tells them:

> Then you are yourselves no longer. You are not Karl Schmitt from Berlin, you are not Anna Kjersk from Kazan, and you are not Peter Sawitch from Moscow. One and all of you are nameless and motherless, blank pages on which the revolution writes its instructions.

With the assumption of masks, the unique identity of each is voided. They do not even have the negative identity of being no one. Their individuality must become flexible, relative, adjustable:

> Then, from this time on, you are no one no longer. From this time on, and probably until you disappear, you are unknown workers, fighters, Chinese, born of Chinese moth-

ers, with yellow skin, speaking Chinese in sickness and in sleep.

Two Agitators speak in chorus: "Yes. The young comrade said Yes too. In this way he agreed to the blotting out of his face." The Young Comrade accepts the logic of that sacrifice of identity but is able to fulfill it only in his death. Ironically, the artifice of the demonstration—the epic distancing—which Brecht employs insures the vital presence of the hero, paradoxically, even in his absence. The Four Agitators, in whose demonstrations The Young Comrade and the other characters are realized, seem anonymous. With the exception of the implicit guilt which directs them to confess to The Control Chorus that they killed a comrade, the playwright does not give them individual feelings. To a great degree, all that we know about them, as individuals is their response to The Young Comrade. The characterization of the hero gains a complexity as each of them shares in the function of demonstrating his behavior. Here, within the psychological complexity which belies the formal simplicity of this play, each of The Four Agitators shares in The Young Comrade's sin. The play, of course, is designed as a lesson—a lesson primarily for those who perform it. The sin expiated in *The Measures Taken* is the surrender to human feeling, and in the mimetic ritual of the dramatized sacrifice, the experience of sacrifice should purge the acute intensity of human feeling. However, the vitality of the hero provides a realism missing in the abstract ethic of The Four Agitators. The demonstration of the sacrifice before The Control Chorus occurs in order to justify the murder of The Young Comrade, but the action seems to exist, on one level, as a ritual of expiation of another kind. The Four Agitators themselves seem to experience guilt, and their confrontation with The Control Chorus seems to be based, at least in part, upon a need to affirm the justice of their action:

We killed him. We shot him and threw him into a lime pit. . . . He often did the right thing. Several times he did the wrong thing. But in the end he endangered the movement. He wished the right thing and did the wrong thing. We demand a verdict.

At the specific moment of the killing The Four Agitators themselves suffer the experience of compassion and their demonstration of the event focuses upon that feeling. Necessity is in conflict with their own compassionate human natures:

> *The time was short, we found no way out.*
> *As one animal will help another, we too*
> *Wished to help him*
> *Who had fought with us for our cause.*

Of course, they sense that compassion as bestial and not rational. Yet it is not easy to accomplish the rational act: "IT IS A FEARSOME THING TO KILL." And they project the responsibility for the offense upon the nature of the world itself:

> *But we will kill ourselves and not just others if necessary*
> *Since only by force can this dying world be changed*
> *As every living man knows.*
> *It is not granted to us, we said,*
> *Not to kill.*

They declare that their own communion with the absolute will of the classical doctrine, allows then no other course: "At one with the will to change the world that will not be denied." The Control Chorus confirms the justice of the action, and they allow their sympathy to be manifested toward the agitators in an expression of their own response to the dilemma realized by the agitators between ultimate necessity and human feeling.

Brecht conceived of this action of the sacrifice of the individual in the same images as those in which he projected his initial vision of the human condition—a world in which man consumes man.

> *Then we shot him*
> *And threw him into the lime pit*
> *And when the lime had devoured him*
> *We returned to our work.*

The poet uses the pervasive image of consumption from the early plays to describe the sacrifice, and this denial of humanity and the devouring of a man is framed in associations which relate to Macheath's justification of crime as the basic process of social existence:

> *What does a man live by? By resolutely*
> *Ill-treating, beating, cheating, eating some other bloke!*
> *A man can only live by absolutely*
> *Forgetting he's a man like other folk!*

However, the ethical scheme of Macheath's declaration is the process of crime, related to the bestial world of Brecht's early nihilism. *The Measures Taken* is a reaction to the nihilistic vision implicit in the early work; and, on one level, it offers an escape from the despair of that vision. It is possible to change the world, to alter reality through

ANGER AND TENACITY, KNOWLEDGE AND INDIG-
    NATION
SWIFT PARTICIPATION, PROFOUND REFLECTION
COLD ACQUIESCENCE, ENDLESS PERSISTENCE
COMPREHENSION OF THE SINGLE MAN AND OF
    THE WHOLE.

This comprehension denies the value of the individual human being; and, in this regard, Ronald Gray is astute in his use of the term, "engineered inhumanity." The play attempts to project the need to maintain the primacy of the whole. However, the vitality of the absent hero and the sense of his death as a devouring, with the underlying sense of guilt implicit in the sacrifice and its confession, keep the resolution of this play from being the patent statement of a polemic. *The Measures Taken* does not succeed in the "comprehension of the single man and the whole"; the dilemma of the play is unresolved, and it remains tragic.

In part, the Marxist Utopia in Brecht's *Lehrstuecke* functions as a symbol, an ideal reality in which man does care for man—in which man is neither exploiter not exploited. That reality could be achieved, in Brecht's mind, by the discipline of Communism. The affirmation of Marxist doctrine was, to Brecht, a means of denying the power of human instinct, the instinct which he sees as destructive.

The satisfaction which Brecht's western audiences have found in the plays testifies to the fact that they transcend the Marxist polemic. It is important to realize that his plays are political in the best sense of the word—and the most profound. The very nature of drama is ethical. The rituals in which drama came into being existed in order to confirm tribal values; and drama serves a major function in affirming the values of society. Brecht is a political playwright, but so, in this sense, are Sophocles and Shakespeare. In one sense, and an important one, both *Oedipus Rex* and *Hamlet* are trials in which fundamental social values are tested and confirmed. Brecht is more explicitly a social playwright, but it is not primarily the Marxist attitude in his plays which makes them political. It is the fact that Brecht uses the theatre as an arena in which to explore man in his relationship with other men; to test the integrity of each personal and social relationship: man and employer; man and state; man and father; man and wife; man and man. Looking at the reality of man and his social institutions, Brecht saw them as destructive, exploitative, and consuming. And it was this despairing vision which made him write about the lack of integrity in man's dealing with man. The atom bomb, its unleashed destruction in Hiroshima and Nagasaki and its potential universal catastrophe, became a symbol to Brecht of what man's social institutions had failed to accomplish. The reverse side of Brecht's despair was a faith in what man could do—if he were free. Within these circumstances, certainly, it is easy to see why Brecht saw the reality of his world primarily in terms of man's exploitation of man. In the world of the early Brecht, the successful man is one who has consumed his fellows—and these works abound with images of feeding, consumption, exploitation. The possibility of a creative relationship between human beings, built upon a scientific foundation, came through the teachings of Marx. The sense of epochal progress, as well, provided an order or at least the possibility of organizing the chaos which Brecht saw in Nature. The teleological quality of Marxism provided the atheist with an ideal, a tangible vessel for his compassion. The asceticism of Communism gave Brecht the control of instinct he desired, and its definite plan for economic and social improvement gave him a means for changing the reality of a world he found to be terrible. In the face of his conception of man as the subject of irrational emotions and instincts, Communism provided a discipline, an ordered process of behavior, in which instincts could be contained and used creatively. And, perhaps most significantly, Communism was for Brecht a means by which his compassion for humankind could be used—attempting to change the causes of suffering. However, *The Measures Taken* demonstrates that while Marxism had given Brecht some sense that the will could be asserted in positive and creative acts, the play also makes clear that this polemic did not offer the poet a complete solution to the struggle of the will against those powers which would restrict it. While the will can assert itself in an altruistic act in *The Measures Taken*, it does so at the cost of its own identity. As the individual human will merges itself with the "will to change the world" it is consumed by the collective.

5

Mother Courage: Instinctive Compassion and "The Great Capitulation"

The didactic Marxist plays, of which *The Measures Taken* is the best, prepared the way for Brecht's greatest dramatic achievements, *Mother Courage, Galileo,* and *The Caucasian Chalk Circle.* In these master works, written while Brecht was in exile from Nazi Germany, the Marxist polemic still operates; however, its function becomes more profoundly philosophic and less definitely political. The plays are still political, but only in the broadest sense of the word. As this study discusses earlier, they are political as they deal with man's relationship with man and question the values of social organization. They seem to disguise their topicality in their use of history or myth, but that disguise is only superficial. *Mother Courage,* a strongly antiwar play, clearly anticipates the world-wide devastation of the Second World War and the futility that Brecht expected would be the consequence of its unlearned lessons. *Galileo,* written before the war but revised in 1945–47, reinterprets history in order to illustrate that modern science is in the unsuitable hands of "Authority" instead of the more creative and, perhaps, beneficent hands of the people. In the revised version, the image of a destroyed Hiroshima stands clear and obvious behind the historical scene. Implicit in these two plays is the destructive consequence of man's exploitation of man—strength, courage, ambition, perception, and intelligence misused by greedy human beings, hungry for the comforts of life despite their cost in human suffering. While it is clear that the superficial disguises of these plays do not mask their topicality, their marked but specific association with the Second World War, it is important to realize that these plays are profoundly universal. They are bold confrontations with the conflict between man's obligations to society and his desire to realize a unique and free identity. While they were written for a certain moment in history, they are explorations of those problems which each age, indeed each man, must solve and resolve continually.

In these master plays the clear form of Brecht's epic structure, which derives from his stated intention of generating an ethical judgment, contains a rich imitation of the vitality and fullness of human experience. While the obvious ethical organization of the works condemns the action of their characters as evil, or as models to avoid, the vitality of these characters, their enjoyment of life and its sensuous comforts, works to provide an ambiguity which complicates the plays but makes them profound explorations of human experience.

The ethical scheme of *Mother Courage and Her Children* is quite clear to anyone familiar with Brecht's dramatic structure. In an earthy and dialectical prose, Brecht relates the story of Anna Fierling, the sutler woman of Grimmelshausen's tale, who lives by her canteen business, following the armies of the religious wars of the seventeenth century. Fierling, the conniving Mother Courage, loses each of her three illegitimate children to the wars. First, Swiss Cheese, a regimental paymaster, is executed by the enemy because he refuses to disclose the whereabouts of his cash box. Eilif is killed for attacking a peasant family during a brief interlude of peace. Kattrin is shot while warning a village of an impending massacre. Mother Courage, whose business has brought her children into the war which eventually kills them, is seen at the close of the play, pulling her wagon after the army, still continuing her business. From the poet's point of view, Anna Fierling, the scheming sutler woman, is unambiguously guilty. In the opening scene, Brecht uses the "Song of Mother Courage" to project an attitude—Anna Fierling's response to war as an arena for commerce. On the narrative level, the song is the hawking cry of the sutler woman; as a *gestus* however, it projects her own use of war and a coldly realistic attitude towards life itself, an honest confrontation with the inevitability of death. The presentation of this image is amplified by the sergeant and the recruiting officer, whose description of conflict extols war as a time of organization and efficiency in which a man can find his identity in fulfilling a useful function.

> What they could use around here is a good war. What else can you expect with peace running wild all over the place. You know what the trouble with peace is? No organization. And when do you get organization? In a war. Peace is one big waste of equipment. Anything goes, no one gives a damn. See the way they eat? Cheese on rye, bacon on the cheese? Disgusting! How many horses they got in this town? How many young men? Nobody knows! They haven't bothered to count 'em! That's peace for you!!! I been places where they haven't had a war in seventy years and you know what? The people can't remember their own names! They don't know who they are! It takes a war to fix that. In a war, everyone registers, everyone's name's on a list. Their shoes are stacked, their corn's in the bag, you count it all up—cattle, men, *etcetera*—and you take it away! [1]

War is a value in the sergeant's attitude because it simplifies exploitation in its efficient use of people and property. His own equivocal sense of honor is revealed as he describes the dishonor of an escaped recruit, who deserted after he had been tricked into enlisting while drunk: "There's no loyalty left in the world, no trust, no faith, no sense of honor." It is demonstrated with some clarity that both Mother Courage and the soldiers are motivated by necessity, committed to the logic of exploitation in order to survive. In their discussion, the nature of Fierling's identity as Mother Courage is defined.

SWISS CHEESE . . . this is Mother Courage!
SERGEANT Never heard of her. Where'd she get a name like that?

EILIF and SWISS CHEESE (*reciting together*) They call her Mother Courage because she drove through the bombardment of Riga with fifty loaves of bread in her wagon!

At this early point Brecht defines her motive: her absolute commitment to business:

MOTHER COURAGE They were getting moldy, I couldn't help myself.

Later in this scene, Anna Fierling's response to the sergeant's demand for papers projects a cynical attitude toward absolute values and the lack of validity in words which form the vows and commitments agreed upon between men.

> Here, sergeant! Here's a whole Bible—I got it in Altötting to wrap my cucumbers in. Here's a map of Moravia—God knows if I'll ever get there. And here's a document saying my horse hasn't got hoof and mouth disease—too bad he died on us, he cost fifteen guilders, thank God I didn't pay it. Is that enough paper?

Again and again in this play, there is an insistence upon the fact that absolute values do not obtain in human experience—even more pessimistically, that one cannot put trust in any human agreement because men are greedy and fickle. Mother Courage herself becomes the clearest image of that greed. Brecht's ethical position is clear in this initial scene: Mother Courage loses her sons to the Recruiting Officer because her impulse to conduct business—to sell the belt to the sergeant—distracts her attention. The final summary speech of this scene contains the central irony of the play:

> *When a war gives you all you earn*
> *One day it may claim something in return!*

The system which sustains Fierling and her family is, in reality, a destructive force to which she also will be subject.

The remaining scenes develop a complicated elaboration of greed as the primary motive of human action. The second scene provides an excellent illustration of the way in which Brecht takes a single episode and builds it into a thematic repetition of a single gesture. The scene begins with Mother Courage at the tent of the Swedish commander, haggling with the cook over a chicken which she wants to sell him. The cook fears the wrath of the commander and, even though he shrewdly disguises this fear, Fierling recognizes it and uses it in her outrageous pricing of the fowl. While haggling there she discovers the commander feting her son because he has captured a group of peasants and, more importantly, their oxen. In the typical Brechtian use of the anecdote, Eilif tells his story.

> It was like this. I found out the peasants had hidden the oxen in a certain wood. The people from the town were to pick them up there. So I let them go for their oxen in peace—they should know better than me where they are, I said to myself. Meanwhile I made my men crazy for meat. Their rations were short already. I made sure they got shorter. Finally, their mouths would water at the sound of *any* word beginning with M—like mother.

Eilif exploits his own men by keeping them hungry—thus making the capture of the cattle an even more desirable objective. It is important that these men act as energetic and efficient soldiers, not from honor, but from hunger. However, as Eilif tells their story, they are overpowered by the peasants. Here Eilif tricks the peasants by appealing to their greed.

> I laughed. And so we got to talking. I came right down to business and said: "Twenty guilders an ox is too much, I bid fifteen." Like I wanted to buy. That foxed 'em. So while they were scratching their heads, I reached for my good sword and cut 'em to ribbons. Necessity knows no law, huh?

In the realistic imagination of the Chaplain who witnesses this scene, virtue is only a possibility when greed has been satisfied: "Our Lord made five hundred loaves out of five so that no necessity should arise. So when he told men to love their neighbors, their bellies were full. Things have changed since his day." In this cynical exposition of a virtue based upon expedience, Brecht has the commander honor the bravery of Eilif. In her discussion with the cook, Courage describes the commander as bad, claiming that a good leader would not need brave soldiers and asserting that ordinary soldiers would be sufficient. She expands upon this thesis by declaring that in a good country such dangerous virtues would be unnecessary: "We could all be cowards and relax." Here there is the concept that the existence of actual virtue and compassion—the state of man living harmoniously with man is a possibility only if man's basic needs are satisfied. The assumption is, of course, that needy man—hungry, cold, or unsatisfied— cannot be virtuous.

At this point Eilif sings the ballad, "The Fishwife and the Soldier," which had been taught to him by his mother. The song begins

> To a soldier lad comes an old fishwife
> And this old fishwife, says she:
> A gun will shoot, a knife will knife,
> You will drown if you fall in the sea.

The content of the ballad insists upon the idea that the identities of people must be fulfilled in certain actions— just as certain objects have their function. If you commit yourself to a soldier's life, you must suffer the consequences of the logic of killing. Ignoring the threat of war, the soldier holds to the promise of his returning: "When the new moon is shining on shingle roofs white / We are all coming back, go and pray for that night!" But, the soldier is swept out by the tide:

> He floats with the ice to the sea.
> And the new moon is shining on shingle roofs white.
> But the lad and his laughter are lost in the night:
> He floats with the ice to the sea.

Ironically, Fierling—who symbolically is the old woman of the ballad—sings the third stanza of the song, and Eilif recognizes his mother. With typical Brechtian clarity, the song defines the relationship of Mother Courage and her son: the old woman who fears the death of the young soldier and the young soldier who is soon to die but who is conscious only of his heroism and present fame. It is also significant that Brecht uses the metaphor of the sea in this song as the symbol of war. The irreversible tide of the ocean is the course of war to which these characters submit; and, like the rivers of the fierce devouring natural world of the early plays, the sea is the force to which the will surrenders. Brecht again sees the acceptance of inevitability in the metaphor of drowning and decaying in water. Here the inevitability is the fatal course of war.

In the first scene, Mother Courage loses her son to the army because she is seduced by the recruiters into conducting business instead of guarding against the threat of induction. In the third scene of this play, in a bold confrontation of reality, Mother Courage haggles over the bribe needed to free the captured Swiss Cheese, and the delay caused by her haggling results in the swift execution of her son. However, Fierling's haggling in the painful experience of Scene Three is an image of far greater complexity than the more simple bargaining of the first scene. It is not a pure greed which motivates the delay that causes the death of Swiss Cheese; the sutler's wagon, which is at stake, is the means of existence for Mother Courage and Kattrin. When she is aware that the cash box is gone, Courage tries to hold on to a sum great enough to "pack a hamper and begin over," declaring "It won't be the end of the world." When she is finally aware of the desperateness of the situation, she is, of course, willing to lose the entire two-hundred guilders, but it is too late. Her faith in the corruption of the businessman-soldier has been too strong:

> I think they'll let us have him. They're not wolves, they're human and after money. God is merciful and men are bribable—that's how his will is done on earth, I don't know about Heaven.

Compassion, in Fierling's imagination, is a matter of purchase. But all human action is not directed by financial transaction. Unwilling to cast all away for the life of her son, Mother Courage loses him. However, her error is not primarily an error in motive but rather an error in judgment—the application of her business *courage* to a situation in which such haggling was inappropriate, indeed, fatal.

> The highly dramatic scene in which Mother Courage loses her honest son Swiss Cheese presents the human conflict intensified as a business conflict. Despite the terrible, knife-edge suspense of the situation, Mother Courage begins to haggle in the moment when she hears that the box with the pay is lost. It is positively terrifying news; it means that Mother Courage cannot buy back the wagon which is to be leased to the camp prostitute Yvette. At first glance the scene has a brutal and inhuman effect. Swiss Cheese dies literally from the margin of difference about which they are haggling. Still, Mother Courage does not haggle for the sake of haggling. Brecht has constructed the situation as a true dilemma. Mother Courage is 'desperate,' as the stage direction notes. She reacts entirely as the 'merchant-mother,' that is, not as a sentimental abstraction, but as a sociologically concrete being when, stifling her first humane impulse, she considers the consequences: the fate of the helpless, mute Kattrin, a life without the wagon, a life without the possibility of living. It is not as though she had thought in the beginning that the life of her son would be risked in the terrible transaction; when the corruptibility of the constabulary turns out to be incorruptible, Mother Courage is ready to pay the whole sum. It is a single moment of reflection which deprives her of her son, just exactly that precautionary prudent 'virtue,' that 'courage,' which is the only thing which up to now has kept her and her children alive through this inhuman war.[2]

With the single exception of Kattrin's compassionate and suicidal act, the primary sense of humanity in *Mother Courage and Her Children* exists in the bond which unites the little family, embodied in Fierling's desperate and futile efforts to hold them together. However, these efforts are made according to a realistic logic in which vows and promises are empty; in which the only bond that unites men is the exchange of items in a commercial transaction.

In her commercial dealings, Courage sees people not as human beings, but in one of two categories: victims and persecutors. And she exercises compassion only in her treatment of Eilif, Swiss Cheese, and Kattrin. There is an irony in the fact that the little human community of Fierling's family is, to a strong degree, seen by Mother Courage as objects which belong to her. They seem to exist for her as commodities. Certainly she has strong feeling for them; yet they seem to her to be things which she owns more than individual and unique beings.

This version of the story of the human will in its futile attempt to assert itself is, perhaps, the most pessimistic telling of the typical Brechtian drama. In a sense *Mother Courage* begins with the human will of Fierling already contained, already disciplined by the human condition. For the will to survive, in this world vision, it must conduct business with courage, as the play defines these terms. Fierling's will has adapted to that logic: it never asserts itself outside the bounds of the rationale of capitulation. In the key song of the play, "The Great Capitulation," Mother Courage describes her loss of innocence, her recognition of the nature of the human condition in which the individual will cannot assert itself, only capitulate. The proverbial affirmations of individual human ability—"Where there's a will, there's a way . . . You can't hold a good man down . . . We can lift mountains"—are played against the realization that only by compromise and acceptance of the futility of individual action can one endure. Mother Courage sings that once she saw herself as unique, exceptional, and capable of asserting an individual will, but that she learned to submit to authority:

(I am the master of my fate. I'll take no orders from no one.)
Then a little bird whispers!

> *The bird says: "Wait a year or so*
> *And marching with the band you'll go*
> *Keeping in step, now fast, now slow,*
> *And piping out your little spiel.*
> *Then one day the battalions wheel!*

> *And you go down upon your knees*
> *To God Almighty if you please!"*

The claim of power and self-direction—"I am the master of my fate"—is replaced in the next stanza with "You must get in with people. If you scratch my back, I'll scratch yours. Don't stick your neck out!" This song of submission is sung in order to convince the Young Soldier that his rage is insufficient to accomplish anything. The poor young man saved the Colonel's horse and is protesting that his captain has kept the reward. Certainly there is within Fierling's imagination a sense that the human will could accomplish a unique and significant action, if its rage were great enough; but she admits that it is more profitable to capitulate to this kind of authority. In Fierling's terms, this capitulation is a submission, an acceptance of the logic of one human being using another. In a larger sense, it is her acceptance of war as a fact of human existence, a way of life which brings her food, shelter, and comfort. Her "Great Capitulation," which is one perspective of her acceptance of the business of war, killing and plunder, ironically makes her more vulnerable to the possibility of losing her family to war.

Surely "The Great Capitulation" is a statement of Brecht's central drama: the futile assertion of the will which learns that it must submit, capitulate, or consent to the energies of an irrational natural world, to the logic of man's exploitation of man, or to the defined ethic of the collective. The dramatic action of Fierling's song is not an assertion but an accommodation, accepting the rhythm of the mass, marching with them, and giving up one's individual desires for happiness as vain or futile. The injustices and deprivation of the human condition, symbolized in the captain's extortion of the young soldier's reward, could only be altered by a "great anger." Here there is a sense of the possibility of a significant human action, generating from the energy of the will. However, in the play itself there is only one such action: the suicidal assertion of the will of Kattrin, an act generated from a "great anger."

Mennemeier makes a perceptive and significant comment about Kattrin in his essay on *Mother Courage*: "The girl, who is obsessed by an animal-like drive for love and motherhood, who suffers from compassion, must never be played as an idiot. Kattrin is completely normal. It is the world that is abnormal, which has terribly deformed her. Because of her 'friendliness' Kattrin—what a symbol!—must be constantly watched. She has only her mother's shameless art of living to thank that she exists at all in the middle of war and business and has even become twenty-five years old. Kattrin is only human and absolutely 'incompetent'; consequently she exists in constant mortal danger."[3] Here is the location of the paradox which gives *Mother Courage* such intellectual and emotional vitality. Kattrin is, certainly, as Mennemeier notes, absolutely vulnerable; and she must be watched, protected, and guarded from exploitation. However, in her total commitment to compassion, she is the only person who possesses the strength of will, the "anger" great enough to accomplish a compassionate and virtuous action.

War, in Bertolt Brecht's epic imitation of the religious wars of the seventeenth century, becomes a metaphor for business. In Brecht's terms, the war itself is the business of the big men who manipulate politics for their own advantage, exploiting mankind, and this ethic of exploitation pervades the social structure, making man's relationship with man primarily a business relationship. Brecht's image of the war as big business is clarified in a conversation between Mother Courage, the chaplain, and the cook. Peter Piper, the virile cook, declares: "And King Gustavus liberated Poland from the Germans. Who could deny it? Then his appetite grew with eating, and he liberated *Germany* from the Germans. Made quite a profit on the deal, I'm told." Courage responds:

He'll never be conquered, that man, and you know why?
We all back him up—the little fellows like you and me.
Oh yes, to hear the big fellows talk, they're fighting
for their beliefs and so on, but if you look into it,

you'll find they're not that silly: they do want to
make a profit on the deal. So you and I back them up!

This principle of profit extends from the "big" King Gustavus to the "little" Mother Courage who ekes out her
existence in her deceitful commerce, her parasitical attach-
ment to the war. As mentioned earlier *Mother Courage
and Her Children* is a repetitious elaboration of the exploitation. The Recruiting Officer and the Sergeant are
searching out soldiers for profit; Courage is using the war
for trade; the numerous soldiers with whom she deals are
selling the supplies of the army to her, illegally, for a
profit; Yvette is engaged in prostitution for profit; the
Chaplain, the Cook, the Captain, the peasants of Scene xi
are all seeking profit from situation of war. In their guilt,
they refer to the time of peace as a time in which ethical
values existed; in the past, before the war, and in the
future,—perhaps—you can live in peace and practice those
virtues which the war causes you to ignore. In the wartime
struggle to survive, man must exploit his fellow man in
order to grasp a sufficient income with which to live.
Ethics can be employed in man's dealings with man only
when his essential needs are met. And, yet, in terms of the
play, war is the given human condition. In Fierling's
"Song of the Great Capitulation," we have the sense that
the "great anger" needed to oppose the war, the "sacrifice" Brecht asked for in the *Couragemodell* is, perhaps,
an action within a Utopia which will never be reached.
The Chaplain sings:

Peacemakers shall the earth inherit:
  We bless those men of simple worth.
Warmakers have still greater merit:
  They have inherited the earth.

I'll tell you, my good sir, what peace is:
  The hole when all the cheese is gone.
And what is war? This is my thesis:
  It's what the world is founded on.
War is like love: it'll always find a way. Why should it end?

After this celebration of war, Mother Courage finds her daughter attacked and wounded, permanently disfigured by the soldiers. Kattrin has been made mute, disfigured, raped by war. Only at this point does Anna Fierling cry out against the life to which she has committed her family:

> And this is war! A nice source of income, I must say! . . . She's finished. How would she ever get a husband now? And she's crazy for children. Even her dumbness comes from the war. A soldier stuck something in her mouth when she was little. I'll never see Swiss Cheese again, and where my Eilif is the Good Lord knows. Curse the war!

Despite this curse, Courage cannot cut herself free from her parasitical dependence upon the war. She is distraught when "peace has broken out" and she is left with a wagonload of goods in a deflating market: "Dear old peace has broken my neck. On the chaplain's advise I went and bought a lot of supplies. Now everybody's leaving, and I'm holding the baby." In this brief moment during the confusing transition from war to peace, Eilif is executed for attacking a peasant's family to plunder the livestock. His action which was "heroic" in wartime is criminal in peacetime, and Eilif, whose ethic has been forged in war, is unable to distinguish the difference, motivated as he was by hunger. His greed, which is a military value in wartime because it satisfies his commander's greed as well, does not function as a value in peacetime. However, Courage is unaware that she has lost her second son; and with the return of wartime business, she celebrates the war as a protective institution, one which supplies and cares for its people, providing as it does ample opportunity for exploitation and plunder:

> *Up hill, down dale, past dome and steeple,*
>   *My wagon always moves ahead.*
> *The war can care for all its people*
>   *So long as there is steel and lead.*
> *Though steel and lead are stout supporters*
>   *A war needs human beings too.*
> *Report today to your headquarters!*
>   *If it's to last, this war needs you!*

However, this caring and protection is a consumption—the war cares for human lives as it devours them; human lives are its raw material.

To read *Mother Courage* primarily as an antiwar poem is a mistake, limiting its significance and its relationship to the Brechtian canon. The state of war in this play is the state of the human condition: it is the greed and exploitation of the cities of Chicago and New York as they exist in *In the Jungle of the Cities*; it is the organized destruction of identity in *A Man's a Man*; the exploitation of the suffering proletariat in *The Measures Taken*. In this world, the assertion of the will in an honest action is suicidal. Swiss Cheese, who is not sufficiently intelligent to be deceitful, refuses to disclose the whereabouts of the regimental cashbox to the enemy, thereby remaining honorable and suffering death. Kattrin, of course, makes the strongest assertion against the exploitation of the war and is destroyed. In this version of Brecht's drama of the human will in conflict with the powers external to it, the assertion of the will is seen as a value, a goodness which cannot survive in this world. However, in that Brechtian dream of a world changed, the action of Kattrin promises a kind of human behavior in which compassion can be exerted and survive.

The image of Anna Fierling, the Mother Courage who has lost all three children to the destructiveness of war, strapped to her wagon in order to go forward once more into her life of trade, prompted the sympathy of Brecht's audiences and irritated the playwright who saw so clearly that Fierling was the focus of an unambiguous guilt.

We felt that the tradeswoman's voluntary and active participation in the war was made clear enough by showing the great distance which she has travelled to get into it. From a number of press notices, however, and a lot of discussions with members of the audience it appeared that many people see Courage as the representative of the 'little people' who get 'caught up' in the war because 'there's nothing they can do about it,' they are 'powerless in the hands of fate,' etc. Deep-seated habits lead theatre audiences to pick on the characters' more emotional utterances and forget all the rest. Business deals are accepted with the same boredom as descriptions of landscape in a novel. The 'business atmosphere' is simply the air we breathe and pay no special attention to. In our discussions war was always cropping up in this way as a timeless abstraction, however hard we might try to present it as the sum of everybody's business operations.[4]

Brecht blamed the première production of the play in Zurich for the image of war as a "natural disaster, an unavoidable blow of fate." In his criticism of this interpretation, Brecht claims that Fierling's willingness to use war is not an " 'eternally human way of behaving.' " It is important to realize that, while Brecht used war as a metaphor for the "human condition," he saw this consuming and egotistic state of society as a highly organized social structure—the condition desired by selfish and greedy mankind. However, in terms of the Brechtian central drama of the will, war as the human condition is a rational way of adapting to the world.

In the powerful eleventh scene, Brecht projects a single action of protest against this consuming, destructive logic of war in which people have become mere commodities for purchase and use. Kattrin's act is the single strong ethical assertion of the play; it is, of course, suicidal. Her "great anger," aroused by a strong compassion, is sufficient for her to resist "The Great Capitulation." It is clear throughout the play that capitulation is primarily a means of self-preservation. Kattrin, however, values the lives of the children of Halle more than her own existence. Unlike all others in this Brechtian world of exploitation and greed, Kattrin is not concerned primarily with herself. Her instinctive energy is directed toward loving and being beloved.

In this scene, Mother Courage has left Kattrin at a farmhouse with a peasant family while she has gone into town to trade, "buying up stocks because the shopkeepers are running away and selling them cheap." The farmhouse is invaded with Catholic troops who reveal that they are

planning to lay siege to the town of Halle. The peasants
lament because they have grandchildren who will be killed
in the attack, but fearing for their own lives and posses-
sions, they are unwilling to endanger themselves in giving
warning. Kattrin leaves them while they are in the midst
of prayer, takes a drum from the wagon, climbs to the
rooftop, and begins beating the drum. The soldiers return,
and when they are unable to convince her to come down,
shoot her. However, as the scene ends, noise comes from
Halle, clarifying that her warning has been heard and that
the city is saved. The scene is clearly structured to define
Kattrin's action as the embodiment of a pure compassion
in clear contrast to the selfish greed and egoism of the
peasants—and implicitly in contrast to the conniving
"courage" of her mother, Anna Fierling.

When they suffer the initial threat of the soldiers, the
peasants are tricked into aiding them by the threat of
losing their livestock—even the life of their son is of less
importance to them than their cattle, their means of
living. The livestock in this scene functions analogously to
Mother Courage's canteen business, her trade. Kattrin's
action of getting the drum, climbing to the roof, and
beginning the beating of the drum is played in counterpoint to the hypocritical prayer of the peasant couple. The
peasants attempt to get her to pray with them, for they
realize that if they do anything to warn the village of the
coming slaughter they will be "cut down for it." And they
justify their inaction to themselves in the prayer offered by
the peasant woman.

> There's nothing we can do. . . . Pray, poor thing, pray!
> There's nothing we can do to stop this bloodshed, so even
> if you can't talk, at least pray! *He* hears, if no one else does.
> . . . Heavenly father, hear us, only Thou canst help us or
> we die, for we are weak and have no sword nor nothing; we
> cannot trust our own strength but only Thine, O Lord; we
> are in Thy hands, our cattle, our farm, and the town too,
> we're all in Thy hands, and the foe is nigh unto the walls
> with all his power.

The peasant couple uses the prayer as a means to justify
their inaction, their selfish self-concern; and instead of

celebrating the compassionate act of Kattrin—which, indeed could have been the answer to their prayer—they are enraged by her action because it puts them in danger. They plead with her to stop; they beg her to have pity for them. They do not care as much for their grandchildren in the town as they do for their own safety: "Have you no pity, don't you have a heart? We have relations there too, four grandchildren. If they find us now it's the end, they'll stab us to death!"

Kattrin's action takes great strength. She focuses all her compassion, the energy she would have brought to being a mother herself, upon an act which is to save all the children of Halle. However, in Brecht's central drama of the will, such an assertion must be suicidal; the human will cannot commit such an act without destroying itself. Kattrin has of course been vulnerable to such destructively compassionate behavior all along, but Mother Courage has been present to protect her from her own instinctive movement toward love. In the ambiguity of the Brechtian drama, Kattrin's assertion is both an assertion of the will and a surrender to instinct. Indeed, Anna Fierling's success in dealing with the world—her courage—comes from her denial of the feelings which Kattrin cannot deny. From Brecht's ethic, Anna Fierling, Mother Courage, does not resist the war, she accomodates and uses it. It is this accommodation which Brecht decries. In the *Couragemodell*, Brecht asks: "WHAT IS A PERFORMANCE OF MOTHER COURAGE AND HER CHILDREN PRIMARILY MEANT TO SHOW?" And he answers: "That in wartime big business is not conducted by small people. That war is a continuation of business by other means, making the human virtues fatal even to those who exercise them. That no sacrifice is too great for the struggle against war." [5] Interestingly enough, there is the same tension between reason and folly in *Mother Courage* as there is in Shakespeare's *King Lear*. The egoistic greed of the rational Edmund, Goneril, and Regan is opposed to the sweet folly of Cordelia's love which does not consider the self-destructive consequences of caring for another. The rational evil of war, embodied in the greed of Mother Courage, is opposed to the compassionate and suicidal action of Kattrin. In *King Lear*, the protagonist learns the ultimate wisdom of caring for another; yet the tragic consequence of the suffering of Anna Fierling is exactly the opposite: she learns nothing at all, and with neither comfort nor wisdom, she commits herself once more to the destructive ethic of business.

The explicit polemic, the clear ethical organization of the play, seems starkly clear and Brecht's frustration at an audience who identified with the suffering Fierling is certainly understandable. And yet, wherein Shakespeare's tragedy it is sufficient to see the consciousness of Lear accepting the ultimate wisdom of moving toward another in love and accepting the care of another human being, in Brecht's *Mother Courage* the final focus is not upon the matured consciousness. In this play the moment of goodness exists in the brief moment at the end of Scene xi when we recognize that Kattrin's act has been successful; and while that value exists within our imagination, there is no comforting sense that it is anything but a unique experience—the single moment of compassion within an exploitative world. There is some indication that in Brecht's imagination, Kattrin's compassion is related to the instinctive weakness suffered also by The Young Comrade in *The Measures Taken*, and, in that sense, her compassionate act is a submission as well as an assertion. However, as the alternative behavior to that of Courage, as the good act which defines the evil of the sutler woman, it is not sufficient to promise the possibility of a better world. In clearer terms, while compassion must be exceptional under the conditions of war, it can never be sufficiently typical to make a strong enough promise of the possibility of peace.

Brecht intended both *Galileo* and *Mother Courage* to be uncomforting explorations of human guilt: "ideological structures" in which the relentless logic of exploitation could be clarified and seen for what it is. In the playwright's conscious mind, the explicit polemic was clear. However, it is important to see that the polemic, in the poet's imagination, built upon a sense of justice which the audience brought to the theatre. Consider the following excerpt from a dialogue with Friedrich Wolf:

> It is not true, though it is sometimes suggested, that epic theatre (which is not simply undramatic theatre, as is . . . sometimes suggested) proclaims the slogan: "Reason this side, Emotion (feeling) that." It by no means renounces emotion, least of all the sense of justice, the urge to freedom, and righteous anger; it is so far from renouncing these that it does not even assume their presence, but tries to arouse or to reinforce them. The 'attitude of criticism' which it tries to awaken in its audience cannot be passionate enough for it.[6]

However, the audiences do not cry out against Anna Fierling, testifying to her use within the play as a pure symbol of human greed and exploitation. Brecht defined the lesson of *Mother Courage* clearly in the same dialogue:

> The play in question shows that Courage has learnt nothing from the disasters that befall her. The play was written in 1938, when the writer foresaw a great war; he was not convinced that humanity was necessarily going to learn anything from the tragedy which he expected to strike it. . . . But even if Courage learns nothing else at least the audience can, in my view, learn something by observing her. I quite agree with you that the question of choice of artistic means can only be that of how we playwrights give a social stimulus to our audience (get them moving). To this end we should try out every conceivable artistic method which assists that end, whether it is old or new.[7]

Implicit, of course, in Brecht's polemic is a sense of the freedom of the human will to assert itself, a freedom which, related to the collective, assumes that the world—the social structure of man with man—can be changed. The poetic complexity of Brecht's work—that which makes it both profound and, sometimes, equivocal—derives from a sense of the human will as the victim of the human condition, the victim of a world in which there is no freedom for the human will. Of course, as this study has discussed the plays, that struggle becomes the central drama of the Brechtian canon.

In many ways, the directing ethic of *Mother Courage* is more explicit, more directly the cause of its structure, than any other of Brecht's masterpieces. Surely it does not take the most perceptive critic to realize that Brecht intended Anna Fierling, Mother Courage, to be the focus of an acutely realized guilt. Fierling is responsible for the deaths of her three children. She has attempted to preserve her little family from the destructive nature of war at the same time in which she has sustained them by trading upon the war in her commercial enterprises. The final image of the play projects the image of the childless mother pulling her own wagon in circles—in literal terms—proceeding with her business, enduring despite her suffering. In Brecht's imagination, she can endure because she has not realized her guilt; and it was difficult for the playwright to see how the audience could interpret this endurance as the justification for her name, Mother Courage. Her courage to endure, to remain "in business," is, on one level certainly, a callous indifference to just what that business means as the embodiment of her own attitude toward human beings. Brecht interpreted the sympathy which his audiences felt as the result of a production style in which the audiences were able to identify with the protagonist.

Certainly the emotional depth of the play derives from its ambiguity; despite his intention Brecht projects a world in which to survive is to exploit. The single action which illustrates the possibility of goodness, of compassion, is Kattrin's suicidal warning of the villagers of Halle. However, in this Brechtian world, to love and to survive are impossible; one denies the other. In our response to the play, we affirm and celebrate the value of Kattrin's compassionate act; and, interestingly, Brecht accepted this identification in the service of his polemic:

> The scene with the drum particularly stirred the spectators.
> . . . Members of the audience may identify themselves
> with the dumb Kattrin in this scene; they may get into her

skin by empathy and enjoy feeling that they themselves have the same latent strength. But they will not have experienced empathy throughout the whole play.[8]

The logic of exploitation directs the action of the play and from a significant point of view, Kattrin's action is possible because she lacks the strength to operate on that logic. She is vulnerable to compassion and must be protected from her own goodness. This play contains the equivalent complexity of The Young Comrade in *The Measures Taken*. Compassion becomes the energy of instinct to which it is difficult not to succumb. Reason, in this play, becomes explicitly the evil, the denial of compassion. In the *Lehrstuecke*, reason is identified with the ethic of the collective, the abstract ideal of the Communist Party. In this version of Brecht's central drama, the complexity which was implicit in the little didactic plays becomes much more obvious. The strict, ascetic reason which controlled and channelled the free-wheeling or chaotic instinct of the earlier plays becomes an evil in itself. The conscious effort to survive becomes a factor operating upon the human will. In *Mother Courage*, the primary will is not Anna Fierling's but rather Kattrin's own instinctive movement toward love and motherhood. But this very instinctive movement has made her vulnerable to exploitation, and she is made mute, disfigured, and eventually killed by the rationalists who see that survival depends upon the use of others.

6

The Life of Galileo: The Focus of Ambiguity in the Villain Hero

Brecht intended Galileo to be a consummate villain, and he would, in all probability have agreed with Harold Hobson's critical assertion: "As in one view humanity is saved by the grace and death of Christ, so in Brecht's, by the life and disgrace of Galileo, humanity is damned." [1] Brecht himself considered his Galileo to be a hero-villain in the tradition of Shakespeare's evil protagonists: "He [Galileo] should be presented as a phenomenon, rather like Richard III, whereby the audience's emotional acceptance is gained through the vitality of this alien manifestation." [2] Brecht's phrase, "the vitality of this alien manifestation," is a concise and perceptive definition of the spectator's emotional reaction to Shakespeare's villain, but while Shakespeare's characterization is complex, *Richard III* is more purely evil and less ambiguous than Brecht's *Galileo*. Despite the magnitude of Galileo's sin, the literal condemnation of his evil in Brecht's polemic is complicated by the fact that his insatiable appetite for life is both the source of his genius and his essential human weakness. Brecht's image of Galileo's appetite is ambiguous. In the metaphoric structure of the play, Galileo's appetite is the motive for his acquisition of scientific knowledge; in a sense, he consumes truth for the pleasure of its consumption. But his appetite for the pleasures of life, both intellectual and sensual, makes him unable to sacrifice himself to demonstrate the integrity of the truth he seeks. The tension between Galileo's hunger for life and his hunger for truth results in a tragic paradox, and

Brecht's firm declaration that *The Life of Galileo* does not contain a tragic action does not alter the implicit tragedy of his conception of the recantation.

The work of the New Criticism has defined ambiguity as a primary value in poetry; and the encounter with the verbal puzzle or the ethical contradiction is now seen as a most profound and meaningful experience between poem and reader. Discussing a "clear case of the Freudian use of opposites" in Hopkins' *The Windhover, to Christ Our Lord*, William Empson states:

> two things thought of as incompatible, but desired intensely by different systems of judgments, are spoken of simultaneously by words applying to both; both desires are thus given a transient and exhausting satisfaction, and the two systems of judgment are forced into open conflict before the reader. Such a process, one might imagine, could pierce to regions that underlie the whole structure of our thought; could tap the energies of the very depths of the mind.[3]

Empson's own teacher, I. A. Richards, has defined tragedy, "perhaps the most general, all-accepting, all-ordering experience known," as the accommodation of opposites: hence the supreme ambiguity. Richards writes: "What clearer instance of the 'balance or reconciliation of opposite and discordant qualities' can be found than Tragedy. Pity, the impulse to approach, and Terror, the impulse to retreat, are brought in Tragedy to a reconciliation which they find nowhere else. . . . Their union in an ordered single response is the *catharsis* by which Tragedy is recognized, whether Aristotle meant anything of this kind or not."[4] In the "Preface to the Second Edition" of *Seven Types of Ambiguity*, Empson quotes extensively from James Smith's strongly negative review of the first edition of his study of ambiguity. Smith does not find Empson's application of ambiguity relevant to the criticism of drama, and he claims that "the first business of the student of drama, so far as he is concerned with ambiguity, is historical; he records that situations are treacherous, that men are consciously or unconsciously hypocritical, to such or such a degree."[5] Bertolt Brecht's critical theories concerning the function of the theatre make it seem likely that Brecht, the critic, would agree with the critical response of James Smith. In fact, the primary function of the epic theatre seems to be to serve as an arena for demonstrations which will invoke not only an ethical judgment but an ethical action. The "Short Organum for the Theatre" insists that dramatic action exists to demonstrate the weakness and injustice of human society which, by rational processes, can be clarified and relieved: "The 'historical conditions' must of course not be imagined . . . as mysterious Powers (in the background); on the contrary, they are created and maintained by men (and will in due course be altered by them). It is the actions taking place before us that allow us to see what they are." [6]

Brecht's attitude toward dramatic action and his strong reaction against the interpretations of his own poetry in terms of depth psychology put Brecht the critic in direct opposition to the kind of criticism practiced by people like Empson and Richards, in which the suspension of the ambiguities is considered to be more valuable than the production of a clear ethical judgment. The exploration of ambiguity in a work of art assumes the presence of both conscious and subconscious processes working in the creative experience. But Brecht's own aesthetic is suspicious of the influence of images from the subconscious. He desired a supremely conscious art, one directed by ethical judgment which also generated an ethical judgment in the conscious attention of the spectator. He wrote: "The subconscious is not at all responsive to guidance; it has as it were a bad memory." [7] Martin Esslin discusses this suspicious attitude toward the influence of the subconscious: "But if a poet like T. S. Eliot wisely acknowledges the mystery behind his own poetic activity, and therefore declines to explain what he *intended* his poetry to mean, Brecht obstinately refused to acknowledge that there was more in what he wrote than the rationally calculated effects he had wanted to achieve. This attitude, which sprang from Brecht's highly complex personality, had very curious results. As he refused even to consider the presence of subconscious emotional factors in his poetry, he could not and did not control it, so that the subconscious elements are, if anything, *more* clearly visible in Brecht's work than in that of poets who understand, and are therefore able to conceal, their subconscious impulses." [8]

As Esslin discusses the matter, Brecht the poet could not create without ambiguity; and while Brecht the critic and theoretician may have demanded explicit clarity, Brecht the functioning poet and playwright produced ambiguous poems. Even *The Measures Taken,* the most didactic of the *Lehrstuecke,* maintains a double perspective in spite of the clear intention of the poet. In the ethical structure of this explicit play, the sacrifice of The Young Comrade is seen as an action which is necessary, and logically determined, for the achievement of an ultimate good.

And yet, in the dialectic conflict between the immediately compassionate act and the maintenance of a distant ideal, the vital humanity of The Young Comrade who cannot reconcile the present act and the ultimate end questions the ethic which demands their separation. Significantly, it is not The Young Comrade himself who questions that ethic; it is the tension between the demands of a specific sense of compassion and an absolute ideal within the play itself which qualifies the acceptance of the comrades' execution of their fellow worker. Martin Esslin writes: *The Measures Taken* is "a devastating revelation of the tragic dilemma facing the adherents of a creed that demands the subordination of all human feeling to a dry and abstract ideal." [9] In his discussion of the tension in Brecht's work as the result of a conflict between reason and instinct in the poet himself, Martin Esslin sees Brecht's motive of the split personality as an expression of this conflict. In an interesting and perceptive critical essay, Walter H. Sokel develops Esslin's point in his consideration of the theme of split personality as a means of clarifying "his deep-seated though oft-denied sense of the tragic." Sokel finds this motive working directly in *A Man's a Man,* the ballet *Seven Deadly Sins, The Good*

Woman of Setzuan, and *Puntila.* He notes: "Indirectly schizoid behavior forms an essential aspect of *Mother Courage* and an important one in *Galileo.*" [10] In *Galileo,* as in *Mother Courage,* the split is not actually dramatized but instead it exists in the tension between Galileo the altruistic scientist who holds the vision of a world freed from limitation by science and Galileo the human being whose sensual appetites demand satisfaction.

While Brecht the polemicist considered *Galileo* in terms of a clear literal meaning, Brecht the poet responded to the human action in the building of a complex verbal structure. It is the potential meaning in the complexity of the verbal structure, as an extension of the literal meaning, to which people like Empson and Richards refer in their use of "ambiguity." Allen Tate says "we may begin with the literal statement and by stages develop the complications of metaphor: at every stage we may pause to state the meaning so far apprehended, and, at every stage the meaning will be coherent." [11] In *Galileo,* that "coherent meaning" includes a realization that Galileo's human appetite includes an insatiable desire for knowledge and, as well, that his recantation, which denies the validity of that very knowledge, is motivated by his desire to avoid pain and continue to satisfy his appetites, both intellectual and sensuous. Galileo the scientist is subject to the demands of Galileo the human being. Galileo's guilt, consequently, is not the clear matter of Brecht's polemic. His character is ambiguous, and this essay intends to explore that ambiguity.

As I noted above, Brecht claimed that the audience's acceptance of Galileo is gained "through the vitality of this alien manifestation"; and the much discussed process of alienation is related to Brecht's desire that his audience be free enough from emotional involvement to make the ethical judgment that Galileo is a villain. However, the image of Galileo as a human being is so strong that such detachment seems impossible. The very complexity of the character and the play denies that detachment. Consider the following passage from Ernst Kris' essay on "Aesthetic Ambiguity" in relation to Brecht's *Galileo.*

The response is not aesthetic at all unless it comprises a shift in *psychic distance*, that is fluctuation in the degree of involvement in action . . . The aesthetic illusion requires, as was emphasized by Kant, a detachment from the workings of the practical reason. In the drama and novel failure to attain such detachment is manifested in that extreme of identification with the characters which focuses interest and attention solely on 'how it all comes out.' In poetry, the Kantian emphasis on detachment can be expressed by Coleridge's formula of 'willing suspension of disbelief.' More generally, when distance is minimal, the reaction to works of art is pragmatic rather than aesthetic. Art is transformed to pinup and propaganda, magic and ritual, and becomes an important determinant of belief and action. The ambiguities with which interpretation must deal are disjunctive and additive: meanings are selected and abstracted in the service of practical ends.[12]

It is the argument of this essay that the nature of Brecht's play, in Kris' terms, is aesthetic rather than pragmatic—that the spectator responds to the figure of Galileo not only as a "phenomenon" of human evil but also as a human being who shares, with him, the weakness of being human.

In the original version of this play, which was written in 1938 and 1939, while Brecht was in exile in Denmark, Galileo is condemned as a coward in his act of recantation. However, as Gunter Rohrmoser notes, in the first version there is greater emphasis upon Galileo's cleverness as he outsmarts the Inquisition and, under the guise of blindness, completes his work and smuggles it out of the country by a pupil. "Thus the cunning of reason triumphs also in the ethic of the scientist's political action, it is as far ahead of its century as his knowledge is, and causes light to dawn in the darkness of his age." [13] However, there is evidence which would suggest that Brecht composed Galileo with the knowledge that the Nazis were exploiting the science of physics to produce the terrible atom bomb; and while Brecht and Charles Laughton were working on the English translation and revision of the play, the version this essay studies, America exploded the atomic bomb in Hiroshima. Certainly this event related to

Brecht's conception of the action and its meaning, and the sin of Galileo's recantation assumes gigantic proportions in the poet's mind.

> The 'atomic' age made its debut at Hiroshima in the middle of our work. Overnight the biography of the founder of the new system of physics read differently . . . Galileo's crime can be regarded as the 'original sin' of modern natural sciences. From the new astronomy, which deeply interested a new class—the bourgeoisie—since it gave an impetus to the revolutionary social current of the time, he made a sharply defined special science which— admittedly through its very 'purity,' i.e., its indifference to modes of production—was able to develop comparatively undisturbed. The atom bomb is, both as a technical and as a social phenomenon, the classical end product of his contribution to science and his failure to society.[14]

Certainly Brecht's clearly defined purpose in the second version of *Galileo* is to demonstrate the scientist's sin as an historic explanation for the subjugation of science to authority. And this play existed in the playwright's mind, obviously, as a demonstration made in the terrifying context of the ultimate result of that subjugation: the already realized mass-killing of the atomic explosions in Japan and the potential annihilation ahead. This definition of Galileo's action is accomplished through the celebration of both the scientist and his discovery as the potential source of the birth of a new age, an age free from the dogmatic veneration of Rome as the focal point of the Ptolemaic universe—from the dogmatic veneration of any absolute—and through the acutely critical presentation of his failure to realize that birth.

The actual presence of the astronomical model, a construction of the Ptolemaic conception of the earth-centered universe, functions symbolically and realistically in the first scene of *Galileo*. This archaic conception is described in metaphors which oppose freedom.

> Those metal bands represent crystal globes, eight of them. . . . Like huge soap bubbles one inside the other and the stars are supposed to be tacked on them. Spin the band

with the sun on it. . . . You see the fixed ball in the middle? . . . That's the earth. For two thousand years man has chosen to believe that the sun and all the host of stars revolve about him. Well. The Pope, the cardinals, the princes, the scholars, captains, merchants, housewives, have pictured themselves squatting in the middle of an affair like that.[15]

Andrea completes the image in his question: "Locked up inside? . . . It's like a cage." The suggestion that the Ptolemaic schematic is maintained to nourish and sustain the ego of authority is answered in the weak and senile Old Cardinal's use of the same image in a desperate attempt to affirm his own value.

I won't have it! I won't have it! I won't be a nobody on an inconsequential star briefly twirling hither and thither. I tread the earth, and the earth is firm beneath my feet, and there is no motion to the earth, and the earth is the center of all things, and I am the center of the earth, and the eye of the creator is upon me. About me revolve, affixed to their crystal shells, the lesser lights of the stars and the great light of the sun, created to give light upon me that God might see me—Man, God's greatest effort, the center of creation.

In the ethical structure of *Galileo*, the scientist's relative truth is opposed to the absolute dogma of the church, a dogma which, significantly, is not maintained by Christian conviction but rather by the power of the capitalistic aristocracy which would collapse if dogma lost its authority. The conflict of the Copernican concept of the universe and the Christian concept of a creating God provides, in essence, only a minor aspect of the conflict of *Galileo*. However, it does exist at certain points; for example: after being shown the stars of Jupiter, Sagredo asks Galileo insistently, "Where is God then. . . . God? Where is God?" Galileo angrily answers: "Not there! Any more than he'd be here—if creatures of the moon came down to look for Him!" Sagredo cries: "Where is God in your system of the universe?" and Galileo's answer is significant: "Within ourselves. Or—nowhere." Even the Little Monk, in an attempt to convince Galileo and himself, does not argue from theology but from psychology, believing that the Christian conception gives meaning to his parents' otherwise pointless existence. The intellectual assumptions of Brecht's *Galileo* deny the existence of God; consequently, since the conflict which produced the play exists apart from a theological motive, Brecht assumes that Galileo is opposed, not from a theological motive, but from a political one. This opposition is defined in Brecht's use of Ludovico to represent Galileo's real enemy—the moneyed aristocracy. Galileo's real confrontation with the opposition comes when Ludovico forces him to decide between a commitment to scientific freedom and the compromise of silence which he has maintained for eight years. Galileo's conflict with the authorities of the church is one level removed from the essential conflict. Barberini's rationality could accommodate Galileo's truth within the church, but—as Pope Urban VIII—he is subject to the pressures of the aristocracy. And Ludovico's family will sanction the marriage between him and Galileo's daughter only if Galileo continues to be silent. Under the promise of freedom, which the scientist anticipates in the papal reign of Barberini, Galileo commits himself to the integrity of science. Ludovico is well aware of the concentration of real power and his assessment is valid in the dialectic of the play, "the new Pope, whoever he turns out to be, will respect the convictions held by the solid families of the country. . . . If we Marsilis were to countenance teaching frowned on by the church, it would unsettle the peasants." When Ludovico leaves, Galileo, Andrea, and Federzoni continue the definition of the real adversary: "To hell with all Marsilis, Villanis, Orsinis, Canes, Nuccolis, Soldanieris . . . who ordered the earth to stand still because their castles might be shaken loose if it revolves . . . and who only kiss the Pope's feet as long as he uses them to trample on the people." There is sufficient internal evidence within the text of the play to demonstrate that the conflict is not a theological one. And Brecht's own foreword states that he considered Galileo's opposition to be the aristocracy, neither Christian doctrine nor the Church. In order to clarify this conflict in contemporary terms, Brecht's foreword instructs that "the casting of the church dignitaries must be done particularly realistically. No kind of caricature of the Church is intended. . . . In this play the Church represents chiefly Authority; as types the dignitaries of the Church should resemble our present-day bankers and senators." [16] In *Galileo* the theological conflict is always secondary to the political; and Rome opposes Galileo, not because he has banished God from the heavens, but because his banishment of man from the center of the universe threatens the hierarchy of the church and the aristocracy which supports it. The social and economic disintegration which the church and aristocracy fear is demonstrated in the ballad and anarchic revel of Scene IX. After describing the obedient scheme of the sun revolving around the earth and the cardinals around the Pope in a hierarchic organization extending to the revolution of the lowly domestic animals around the servants, in the Great Chain of Being, the ballad singer continues:

Up stood the learned Galileo
Glanced briefly at the sun
And said: "Almighty God was wrong.
In Genesis, Chapter One!"
Now that was rash, my friends, it is no matter small
For heresy will spread today like foul diseases.
Change Holy Writ, forsooth? What will be left at all?
Why: each of us would say and do just what he pleases!
Good people, what will come to pass
If Galileo's teachings spread?
No altar boy will serve the mass
No servant girl will make the bed.
   Now that is grave, my friends, it is no matter small:
   For independent spirit spreads like foul diseases!
   (Yet life is sweet and man is weak and after all—
   How nice it is, for a little change, to do just as one
      pleases!)

The licentious freedom of the pantomime celebrates that promised anarchy.

Perhaps the strongest judgment of Galileo's recantation within the play rests in the brilliant contrapuntal structure of Scene xii, in which his assistants and his daughter await the results of the trial in the garden of the Florentine Ambassador in Rome. Andrea, Federzoni, and the Little Monk reveal their anxiety in their increasingly strong affirmation of their faith in the master's integrity as the moment of trial approaches. Against the counterpoint of Virginia's Latin prayers, prayers made in her acute fear that her father will not recant, they vehemently deny the statement of the informer who claims that at five o'clock the big bell of San Marcus will be rung to announce the recantation. Andrea affirms the truth of Galileo's discovery in a shouted declaration which, ironically, has the sound of a new liturgy: "The moon is an earth because the light of the moon is not her own. Jupiter is a fixed star, and four moons turn around Jupiter, therefore we are not shut in by crystal shells. The sun is the pivot of our world, therefore the earth is not the center. The earth moves, spinning about the sun. And he showed us. You can't make a man unsee what he has seen." Federzoni announces, "Five o'clock is one minute," and Virginia's frenzied prayers intensify. The assistants stand, hands covering their ears, as the moment comes and goes in silence: their tension breaks into joy. Against Virginia's grief and the irony of reality, the assistants express their response to the acute significance of Galileo's gesture. The magnificent integrity, with its potentially infinite meaning to a new age, counteracts their grief at the master's pain or death; and they celebrate his gesture. Federzoni cries: "June 22, 1633: dawn of the age of reason. I wouldn't have wanted to go on living if he had recanted." The Little Monk confesses the agony of suspense and condemns his "little faith" in an association of Galileo with Christ. In the meaningful images of darkness and light, Federzoni sees the recantation, which he no longer fears, as a return to irrationality and ignorance from the promise of reason and truth: "It would have turned our morning to night." And Galileo's potential strength is defined as

Andrea declares in painful irony: "It would have been as if the mountain had turned to water." This celebration is played against Virginia's despair; and at its peak, the bell begins to toll. The counterpoint reverses its rhythm, and the assistants stand in despair against the rejoicing of Virginia. The mountain had turned to water. Galileo enters, and he confronts his assistants, transformed, "almost unrecognizable." In hysterical despair, the center of his idealism dissolved, Andrea cries: "He saved his big gut." To Galileo he says, "Unhappy is the land that breeds no hero"; and Galileo says simply, "Unhappy is the land that needs a hero."

Brecht's attempt to define Galileo's sin explicitly is seen in the obvious structural relationship of Scenes i and xiii. In the first scene, the middle-aged Galileo enchants Andrea, the son of his housekeeper and Galileo's student, with his description of the birth of a new age in which man will break out of the Ptolemaic cage: "There was a group of masons arguing. They had to raise a block of granite. It was hot. To help matters, one of them wanted to try a new arrangement of ropes. After five minutes discussion, out went a method which had been employed for a thousand years. The millennium of faith is ended, said I, this is the millennium of doubt. And we are pulling out of that contraption." Galileo's enthusiasm for the birth of a new age predicts that science will be the possession of the common people, and the arbitrary hierarchy will disintegrate, "in our time astronomy will become the gossip of the market place and the sons of fishwives will pack the schools. . . . By that time . . . they will be learning that the earth rolls around the sun, and that their mothers, the captains, the scholars, the princes and the Pope are rolling with it."

In Scene xiii the birth of the new age is also discussed by Andrea and Galileo; but now it is a discussion between an old Galileo and an adult Andrea, a confrontation of the disillusioned student and the master who betrayed his ideal by selling his science to the authorities. The implicit tension in this confrontation belies Brechtian objectivity.

In his dedication to the search for knowledge, Galileo
kindled a scientific idealism in his young pupil and fellow
scientist. Against the standard of this idealism, a faith in
the freedom of knowledge which he had inculcated, Galileo's realistic action, the compromise of his recantation,
was unacceptable—a betrayal of the very freedom from
dogma which his discoveries promised. In the apparent
simplicity of this confrontation, a sophisticated complexity is working. When Galileo presents Andrea with the
completed *Discorsi* and suggests how the mask of the
faithful Christian has allowed him to complete his work,
the younger man sees the value of Galileo's realism:
"With the crowd at the street corners we said: 'He will
die, he will never surrender.' You came back: 'I surren-
dered but I am alive.' We cried: 'Your hands are stained!'
You say: 'Better stained than empty.' . . . You gained
time to write a book that only you could write. Had you
burned at the stake in a blaze of glory they would have
won." Then Galileo, again assuming the role of teacher,
attempts to counter Andrea's realism with a rekindling of
the idealism he has maintained:

> The practice of science would seem to call for valor. She
> trades in knowledge, which is the product of doubt. And
> this new art of doubt has enchanted the public. The plight
> of the multitude is old as the rocks, and is believed to be as
> basic as the rocks. . . . But now they have learned to
> doubt. . . . As a scientist I had almost an unique opportu-
> nity. In my day astronomy emerged into the marketplace.
> At that particular time, had one man put up a fight, it
> could have had wide repercussions.

Instead, the new age, which began in the ships ventur-
ing freely from the coasts and which could have been
confirmed as the "dawn of the age of reason" at the
moment when Galileo refused to recant, has been transformed into the image of a "whore, spattered with blood."
Rohrmoser notes a significant revision from the original
text to the reworked version by Brecht and Laughton. He
quotes the earlier text: " 'I insist that this is a new age. If
it looks like a blood-stained old hag, then that's what a

new age looks like. The burst of light takes place in the deepest darkness.' " [17] The later text, in the context of the explosion at Hiroshima, reads more ambiguously: "This age of ours turned out to be a whore, spattered with blood. Maybe, new ages look like blood-spattered whores." Brecht's later plays contain a controlled language which is in strong contrast to the richly textured imagery of the early plays and poems. The conscious deliberation of this image is, consequently, very significant. As Rohrmoser's essay on Galileo suggests, and Brecht's introductory remarks confirm, the concept of the new age is a primary concern of the play. And it is vital that Galileo, who sees his own sin with such intense clarity, conceives of the new age in the image of the "blood-spattered whore"—sold and exploited. Implicit in Galileo's image is the idea that Galileo himself has sold the age, which was in his hands, which, purchased and consumed, has become the bloody whore.

The Life of Galileo is not the clear and simple defamation of Galileo's act which the isolation of these images and actions would suggest—and which, according to his own descriptions of the play, Brecht intended it to be. However, what the play loses in the explication of thesis it gains in an increasing profundity in its ambiguity—an ambiguity which sees the action in a complex of perspectives.

This ambiguity is focused in the implicit schizoid structure of its hero. Brecht uses the structural device of the split personality more obviously in a minor character than in the character of Galileo, but he uses it to define the action of compromise which anticipates Galileo's recantation. One of the most dynamic scenes of the play is that in which Barberini, being clothed in the robes of the church, moves from the identity of the Cardinal, sympathetic to science, to the identity of the Pope, opposed to the threat which science presents to dogma and papal security. This transformation is clarified in the stage directions:

> During the scene the POPE is being robed for the conclave he is about to attend: at the beginning of the scene he is

plainly Barberini, but as the scene proceeds he is more and more obscured by the grandiose vestments.

The little scene begins with Barberini's insistent negation of the Cardinal Inquisitor's demands that Galileo be forced to recant, but the Inquisitor's pervasive arguments and the restlessness of the Papal Court, expressed in the noise of shuffling feet, break down Barberini's scientific considerations as he assumes the identity of Pope Urban VIII. As Cardinal Barberini, he can insure that Galileo will neither be executed nor tortured; as Pope Urban VIII, he cannot insure that Galileo will not be threatened.

This transformation relates to another meaningful use of the symbol of the dual personality, integrity and compromise. At the ball at the residence of Bellarmin in Rome, the two Cardinals, Bellarmin and Barberini, charge Galileo, in the guise of friendship, to abandon his teachings. Barberini is sympathetic—already torn between his belief in science and his obligation to the Holy Church. Ironically, the Cardinals approach in masks: Barberini as a dove, Bellarmin as a lamb. The masks are lowered as they discuss and debate with Galileo; but, resuming the guise of social amenity, Barberini comments: "Let us replace our masks, Bellarmin. Poor Galileo hasn't got one." However, in the development of the play, Galileo assumes his mask; and he uses it in much the same manner of Barberini's mask of the dove and the mask of identity as Pope Urban VIII.

While Gunter Rohrmoser responds to the complexities of Brecht's *Galileo*, he insists upon rejecting the idea that the play is concerned "with the interpretative dramatization of a complex character." He continues: "In turning to history Brecht is concerned in substance with the basic historical and human problem of his own age. . . . Galileo does not interest him as a character, but as a case, although the individual vital substance of the hero is not sacrificed to an abstract scheme to the same extent as in the plays of a Marxist cast, the didactic plays." [18] From his

Marxist perspective, surely Brecht saw Galileo's betrayal of science as an historical action which issues in the real and potential horrors of the atomic age. However, in Brecht's poetic imitation of this action, Galileo's failure becomes not exceptional but, on the contrary, essentially human; and, as the focal point of a complex of opposing motives, Galileo embodies human failure. To consume life, with all the pleasures that consumption entails, becomes a stronger motive than to maintain an abstract ideal—if forced to make a choice. And, in the central ambiguity, that ideal is generated in the very appetite for life which demands its sacrifice. The ambiguity extends to another level: while we respond to Andrea's argument that Galileo's cunning has allowed him to complete his work and make an historic gesture even more significant than his sacrifice would have been, we know that the Schweikian acquiescence which assured the continuation of his work did not derive from an abstract dedication to continue performing the birth of a new age. The suggestion of the recantation as a Schweikian trick is present in both of Brecht's major versions of *The Life of Galileo*, but it is not as strong an image in the second. And, it is important to realize that Galileo's continued work is accomplished itself in a compulsive joy of discovery and affirmation of hypothesis, not purely in the altruism of scientific contribution. Galileo does not plot to smuggle the *Discorsi* out of Italy; it is mere chance that Andrea comes. Surely Brecht enjoyed this final irony. While Galileo again assumes the role of idealist to convince Andrea that his master was wrong and is guilty of the separation of science and humanity, he himself—divorced from humanity in his false identity—continues his work, because of his appetite, whether or not it will be realized in application. Brecht creates his Galileo as a man with an incessant hunger for life; Cardinal Barberini, become Pope Urban VIII, declares: "He has more enjoyment in him than any man I ever saw. He loves eating and drinking and thinking. To excess. He indulges in thinking-bouts! He cannot say no to an old wine or a new thought." Brecht's Galileo has an insatiable appetite for knowledge which is only one aspect of a total appetite for life itself, an indulgence in pleasure as well as an attempt to free mankind from the prison of misconceptions in which they are bound. His work is both altruistic and essentially selfish at the same time. He is committed both to the salvation of mankind and his own indulgence in life; and when put to a decision between mankind and life, the division cannot be made—hence the tragic course.

Brecht continually associates Galileo's hunger for food with his hunger for knowledge. Considering the possibility of attaching himself to the Florentine Court of the Medici in order to give himself time for research, Galileo tells the Curator that he is dissatisfied with his position in Venice, but that his primary source of discontent is his lack of scientific achievement: "My discontent, Priuli, is for the most part with myself. I am forty-six years of age and have achieved nothing which satisfies me." His justification to Sagredo and Virginia for the move to Florence, and the compromises a court appointment will bring, is made in other terms: "Your father, my dear, is going to take his share of the pleasures in life in exchange for all his hard work, and about time too. I have no patience, Sagredo, with a man who doesn't use his brains to fill his belly."

The contrast of relationships between Galileo and Andrea in Scenes i and xiii has already been discussed, primarily however, to clarify Brecht's explicit structuring of the conflict. The scenes also relate to the play's ambiguity. Essentially Galileo's schizoid personality is divided into Galileo the scientist and visionary of a new age and Galileo the glutton who satisfies his appetite for food, wine, and ideas in the same indulgence. In order to satisfy his appetite for knowledge, to gain time both for research and physical pleasure, he trades his intellectual freedom. And, at the crucial moment, to avoid pain—again an indulgence in pleasure—he submits to authority, trading the freedom of scientific truth. The specific relationship of these indulgences Brecht saw clearly and identified, not only in the play, but in his commentary on epic acting in "A Short Organum." Discussing the first scene of *Galileo*, he says:

> To play this, surely you have got to know that we shall be ending with the man of seventy-eight having his supper, just after he said good-bye forever to the same pupil. He is then more terribly altered than this passage of time could possibly have brought about. He wolfs his food with unrestrained greed, no other idea in his head; he has rid himself of his educational mission in shameful circumstances, as though it were a burden: he, who once drank his morning milk without a care, greedy to teach the boy. But does he really drink it without a care? Isn't the pleasure of drinking and washing one with the pleasure he takes in new ideas? Don't forget: he thinks out of self-indulgence.[19]

The primary ambiguity of *The Life of Galileo* finds its source in the fact that Galileo's indulgence in life's pleasures generates the appetite for knowledge and hence the knowledge itself, and simultaneously, generates the human weakness which makes him unable to say no to the threat of pain. His submission to appetite is both his strength and his weakness.

I. A. Richards considers tragedy to be "the balance or reconciliation of opposite and discordant qualities," and in *Galileo* we have that balance in this specific ambiguity. Galileo cannot separate the appetite for knowledge, and, consequently, the ideal of scientific freedom, from the appetite for life itself; both are the same. In Brecht's polemic, Galileo should have subordinated one appetite to the other: Galileo the scientist should have triumphed over Galileo the human being, and the ideal of scientific freedom should have been maintained. However, in the schizoid structure of *The Good Woman of Setzuan*, Shen Te cannot maintain the division of herself into the compassionate Shen Te and the efficient realist Shui Ta; neither can she accommodate the unification of the schizoid personality at the conclusion of the action. Galileo himself cannot subordinate one aspect of himself to the other; and *Galileo* ends, as *The Good Woman of Setzuan* ends, with the human personality in conflict with itself.

Brecht himself writes that the appetite for physical pleasure motivated Galileo's capitulation to deceit in the telescope fraud and he claims that this deception leads to Galileo's excitement of discovery, an excitement that brings a satisfaction which is the same as that of physical indulgence. The satisfaction of appetite trains Galileo in the process of compromise. "His charlatanry . . . shows how determined this man is to take the easy course, and to apply his reason in a base as well as a noble manner. A more significant test awaits him; and does not every capitulation bring the next one nearer?" [20]

Galileo is forced to choose between his indulgence in life's pleasures and the retreat from pain and the maintenance of an abstract ideal. The tragic ambiguity remains in the fact that this ideal is meaningful to Galileo only when it relates to his own personal satisfaction; his tragic course is inevitable in the terms in which Brecht has drawn his character.

The sense of tragedy in *The Life of Galileo* grows out of this paradox. Reconsider I. A. Richards' definition of tragedy in its application to Galileo: "Pity, the impulse to approach, and Terror, the impulse to retreat, are brought in Tragedy to a reconciliation which they find nowhere else, . . . Their union in an ordered response is the *catharsis* by which Tragedy is recognized." Galileo suffers acutely from the knowledge that his act of cowardice is the antecedent of terrifying destructive force. The intensity of Galileo's sensuousness, the equation of his indulgence in scientific experimentation and his indulgence in the gratification of physical pleasures, relate him to Brecht's celebration of sensuality, the grotesque Baal. However, Baal cannot comprehend an ethical concept, and Galileo is acutely aware of his ethical responsibility. Galileo experiences "THE COMPREHENSION OF THE SINGLE MAN AND THE WHOLE." However, unlike The Young Comrade in *The Measures Taken*, he is unable to perform the act of "cold acquiescence." The Young Comrade agrees to his own sacrifice with the knowledge that his death is a necessary process in the revolutionizing of the world. Galileo is unable to sacrifice his humanity, but with The Young Comrade he shares an understanding that the birth of a new age is dependent upon his acquiescence and this knowledge engenders in Galileo his painful guilt.

In Scene XIII, Brechtian alienation occurs when the spectators are made aware that Galileo refers to the terrors of the atom bomb when he discusses the gap between science and humanity which his act of cowardice has rendered: "Should you then, in time, discover all there is to be discovered, your progress must then become a progress away from the bulk of humanity. The gulf might even grow so wide that the sound of your cheering at some new achievement would be echoed by a universal howl of horror." This juxtaposition of the historic Galileo and our contemporary knowledge functions to alienate; however, this awareness magnifies Galileo's grief and guilt, especially guilt, to an incomprehensible extreme. Consequently, as spectators, we retreat, in Richards' terms, in terror for a criminal who could really bear no greater guilt. He placed science in the hands of those who used it, in secret, to produce the most extensive destructive force the world has ever seen. However, at the same time as we retreat from the horror of Galileo's action, we pity him as an acute sufferer, the bearer of an immense and destructive guilt. And we recognize that his failure is an essential human failure: a weakness which produced his knowledge and sacrificed it to its source. In this ambiguity, these "opposite and discordant qualities" are suspended in a single response.

The tragic nature of *The Life of Galileo* defeats, to a considerable degree, the explication of its didactic motive. The spectator cannot withdraw from Galileo's action and state: "He should have been willing to sacrifice himself to pain, certainly, even death because he fully recognized the ultimate consequence of his acquiescence to the demands of authority. He should have realized that the strength of his position would have insured his safety." However, the perceptive spectator cannot make this judgment, because for Galileo to deny life would be for him to deny the source of scientific truth; and the Galileo trained in the denial of life could not have been the Galileo whose affirmation of life brought forth his discoveries.

Certainly Brecht's despair which informs, even directs, the early plays was not thoroughly alleviated in the Marxist solutions of the didactic plays. The unredeemed and enduring logic of exploitation, the rational manueverings to survive, which represent Brecht's conception of human behavior are manifestations of a despair rather than affirmations of an idealistic faith in human progress. In *Galileo*, Brecht decries the fact that Galileo did not change the world and yet, in his fallible humanity, Galileo does not have the will to change the world. That world needs to be changed, and that need is clarified in *The Good Woman of Setzuan*, where the unresolvable tension between goodness and survival projects no answer, only a pathetic cry for help. Certainly, *The Caucasian Chalk Circle* is not an apocalyptic translation of Brecht's despair into a rationalization of human goodness, or into a dramatization of a human will which can assert itself in freedom and survive. The corrupt princes, exploiting their people in the war-mongering search for profit, are reminiscent of the greedy capitalists of *St. Joan of the Stockyards*, and the brutal sexuality of the soldiers make them Baal-like in their destructive energy. In other versions of Brecht's central drama, these bestial elements of human nature succeed. That these evils are not triumphant in *The Caucasian Chalk Circle* is not, necessarily, a proof of Brecht's changing vision, but rather an indication of his own instinctive movement toward compassion and his enjoyment of the romance of goodness successful. In responding to the surprisingly happy ending of this play, it is important to realize that the work is contained within the framework of a deliberate romance—that dramatic form in which the poet and spectator enjoy the illusion of a dream realized. In this play, the complex narrative technique maintains the fictitious nature of the action throughout the play. *The Caucasian Chalk Circle* rejoices in the moment of love held suspended within the larger, realistic context of hate and ugliness and mutability. It is significant to realize that the presence of rewarded goodness and the promise of happiness in *The Caucasian Chalk Circle* exist only in the form of a deliberate fiction. The obvious illusion of Brecht's parable seems to suggest that in a world in which compassion and justice exist only momentarily in the larger context of hatred and exploitation, only the poet can celebrate pure goodness and give it an extended reality.

7

The Caucasian Chalk Circle: The Dream of Goodness and Compassion Realized

In *Mother Courage* and *Galileo*, Bertolt Brecht explores human guilt relentlessly, presenting a mother's greed which destroys her family and a scientist so consumed with an appetite for life that he trades the freedom of modern science in exchange for a release from pain and the promise of physical comfort. However, despite the explicit polemic with which the idealist Brecht directs the action of both plays, neither Anna Fierling nor Galileo Galilei suffers a pure unambiguous guilt. In each case, the protagonist is unable, so it seems, to make a clear assertion without destroying himself. Weighing the advantages of survival against the oblivion of death or the pain of suffering, the will opts for a deprived but continuous endurance. Both the sutler woman and the scientist capitulate; they surrender to a world in which exploitation is the rational course of action, the accepted logic. These plays, however, strongly value the refusal to capitulate and the choice to assert the will in an anger directed against the human condition. In *Mother Courage*, the compassionate gesture of Kattrin, who sacrifices herself to warn the villagers of Halle of the impending massacre, is affirmed as the exemplary act of the play. Implicit in Brecht's version of Galileo's recantation is the meaning that his refusal to compromise would have held for mankind, if his will had been strong enough. In the ethical ideal of his humanism, Brecht saw the possibility of a world in which man could live creatively and harmoniously with man; and against this ideal human inadequacies were etched even more sharply. However, Brecht's plays seem to be repeated versions of a situation in which a human being is unable to assert himself because of some power which is external to his own will. While this repeated action is, in one sense, a multiple declaration of the futility of human experience, in which irrational powers prevail, there is present a clear sense of compassion—frequently weak, usually ineffective, and sometimes ironically destructive—but always present to claim that the will is searching for some value outside of its own being.

Instinctive compassion is a major subject of Brecht's last major dramatic work, *The Caucasian Chalk Circle*, which was written in 1944–45 while Brecht lived in exile in the United States. This beautiful play, which is a kind of dramatic dream, concerns a young servant girl who saves the deserted infant child of the Prince during a revolution. The revolution itself has the typical qualities of a Brechtian war: it is motivated by greed and is waged primarily for profit through graft and corruption; the politicians prosper and the common people suffer. In the revolution on Easter Sunday, the Governor's wife, Natella Abashwili deserts her infant son. She is more concerned about escaping with her gorgeous and costly finery than she is about the safety of her child. Grusha Vashnadze, who has just become betrothed to one of the soldiers assigned to guard the fleeing Governor's wife, discovers the abandoned child, escapes with her dangerous cargo, and journeys over the mountains to her brother's home. There she finds it necessary to marry in order to provide shelter and food for the child. When the war is ended, her lover, Simon, seeks her out. But when he finds her married and with a young child, he leaves her, embittered and disillusioned. After the war, the child represents a legacy to its real mother, and the boy is stolen from Grusha. However, after the revolution a licentious and derelict old man, the notorious coward, Azdak, was made a judge. Azdak's judicial wisdom is directed by a curious, absurd, but compassionate logic; he is the magistrate who hears the trial in which Grusha and Natella Abashwili each claim to be the boy's real mother—Abashwili by birthright and Grusha by the care, protection, and love in which she has held and raised the good child. Azdak calls upon the ancient Chinese myth of the chalk circle, draws it upon the ground, puts the boy in the center, and tells each woman to take one hand of the child. He declares that the true mother will be able to pull the child from the circle. Of course, Grusha is unable to pull the child strenuously in her fear that she will hurt the creature whom she loves so dearly. Azdak realizes her love and awards the child to her, the woman whose care has earned him. In a comically grotesque manipulation of justice, he also divorces Grusha and frees her to marry Simon. Completing the naïve and primitive simplicity of this lyrical tale, Simon, Grusha, and Michael become a unified and happy family.

The structure of *The Caucasian Chalk Circle* is a curious combination of the simple, direct, and delicately handled compassion of Grusha's action of caring for the deserted child and the grotesque, bawdy, and devious implementation of compassion in Azdak's reign as judge. Yet the simple purity of the young girl who protects the abandoned child provides the sensual judge with his supreme act of justice; and the absurd misrule of the judge gives the young girl the promise of happiness—the restoration of the child and the opportunity to marry her beloved Simon. And, significantly, both courses of action develop from the chaos of "that Easter Sunday of the great revolt." As the Christian festival celebrates the birth of a new age in which man is given the promise of immortality, the Easter morning of *The Caucasian Chalk Circle* seems to bring forth the possibility of love, compassion, and generosity within a world of hate, exploitation and selfishness.

While compassion is still seen as instinctive energy, the quality of the playwright's response is quite different. The presentation of Grusha Vashnadze is earthy and, in a sense, realistic. But this late characterization is an abstraction of an essential goodness in human nature; and in clear contrast to Brecht's early imitations of compassionate human nature, this goodness is rewarded. The increasing emotional depth and formal control of the later Brecht can be illustrated in comparing the simple, yet profound, characterization of the Grusha of *The Caucasian Chalk Circle* with the poet's conception of the suffering servant girl in "Concerning The Infanticide, Marie Farrar," discussed earlier. Grusha is a lyrical celebration of innocence and love in violent contrast to the sordid, indulgent pity of Brecht's description of the oppressed victim of the early poem. Both are servant girls, deprived and mistreated, accepting their exploitation; in many ways, however, Grusha Vashnadze is the exact antithesis of the heroine of the poem. Marie Farrar carries her unborn child through the long painful work of the day.

> *It was very late when she went up to bed.*
>
> . . . .
>
> *She was sent for again as soon as she lay down:*
> *Snow had fallen and she had to go downstairs.*
> *It went on till eleven. It was a long day.*
> *Only at night did she have time to bear.*[1]

Grusha's innocence contrasts with Marie Farrar's lustful indulgence in sexuality; her loveliness and purity contrast with the unexpected sensuality of the unappealing Marie. And yet, it is important to realize that Marie Farrar's sexual experience is an aspect of her exploitation. In Brecht's conception of a consuming universe, Marie Farrar becomes an object for others' comfort, including sexual use.

> *Often drops of sweat*
> *Broke out in anguish as she knelt at the altar.*
> *Yet until her time had come upon her*
> *She still kept secret her condition.*
> *For no one believed such a thing had happened,*
> *That she, so unenticing, had yielded to temptation.*[2]

Marie Farrar kills her child in the snow-filled latrine, unable in her pain and isolation to bear its cries. Grusha Vashnadze willingly accepts the experience of suffering necessary to protect the child, and she christens her adopted child in the icy water of the glacier stream, pledging him to life.

> *Since no one else will take you, son,*
> *I must take you now.*
> *Since no one else will take you, son,*
> *(O black day in a lean, lean year!)*
> *You must take me.*
> *I have carried you too long*
> *My feet are tired and sore*
> *And the milk cost much too much*
> *I've grown fond of you:*
> *I wouldn't be without you any more . . .*
> *I'll wash you, son, and christen you*
> *In glacier water*
> *You must see it through.*[3]

The early Brecht demands compassion for Marie Farrar, the infanticide, but his creation of Grusha is, in itself, a concentrated symbol of compassion. After the ritual christening, the truth of her adoption of the child is proved in the ordeal of crossing the chasm on the dangerous rope bridge:

> *Deep is the abyss, son,*
> *I see the weak bridge sway*
> *But it's not for us, son,*
> *To choose the way.*

Brecht accomplishes the characterization of the innocent Grusha in a visualization of action in which sentimentality is deliberately restrained in the use of theatrical conventions and in a poetic imagery which is fragile and delicate. The direct honesty and simple innocence of Grusha is demonstrated in the initial scene between the young girl and Simon in which her obvious interest in the young man is temporarily disguised by her indignation aroused by his watching her at the river. And the tenderness of Simon's proposal and her acceptance are brilliantly outlined against the turmoil of the revolution which defines the special value of their vows: a moment of mutual trust and love posed against the hate and exploitation generating the war. Brecht constructed an obviously theatrical scene in the deliberately stylized dialogue in which Grusha and Simon address their love and concern for each other, and yet the restraint of the young lovers seems to grow naturally out of their mutual shyness. This restraint causes them to identify each other in the third person: "the young lady" and "the soldier." This formality gives the betrothal a ritual quality, climaxed by the gift of the cross, a formal simplicity which concentrates upon the profound meaning which these vows hold for each of them. Their use of proverbs seems appropriate to their peasant natures, and yet at the same time, the ambiguous simplicity of the metaphoric proverb gives a depth and profundity to their speech which seems to develop from their intuitive awareness of the value of their love. Their mutual knowledge of each other, which is revealed in this scene, quietly informs them and the spectators of the presence of their love prior to this actual encounter in which its reciprocity is realized.

In *The Measures Taken*, compassion is a temptation to which The Young Comrade succumbs in his inability to suppress instinct. In *The Caucasian Chalk Circle*, when Grusha remains behind with the deserted child, The Story Teller's narrative declares: "Terrible is the seductive power of goodness!" The movement towards compassion in this late play is intuitive but rather than being condemned, as it is in the didactic plays, it is valued. Esslin states:

> Once Brecht had accepted the discipline of this new creed, and the threat of being overwhelmed by uncontrolled instinctive forces had receded, the emotional side appeared in an increasingly sympathetic light. It was as if the guilt feelings that had originally been evoked by the temptation to succumb to subconscious urges were now transferred to the other side: Brecht now felt guilty at having opted for a coldly rational and inevitably cruel ideology.[4]

Grusha's imaginative vision of her compassionate act is contained in The Story Teller's description of the plaintive call which, in her imagination, is made by the abandoned child. Here Brecht's poetic integrity is demonstrated in the objective narrative which uses images uniquely appropriate to the consciousness of the young woman whose imaginative mind is filled with thoughts of her promised soldier.

"Woman," it said, "Help me."
And it went on, not whining, but saying quite sensibly:
"Know, woman, he who hears not a cry for help
But passes by with troubled ears will never hear
The gentle call of a lover nor the blackbird at dawn
Nor the happy sigh of the exhausted grape-picker as the
*   Angelus rings."*

In the deliberate clarity of the naïve separation of good and evil in *The Caucasian Chalk Circle*, Brecht affirms the Christian doctrine that the good life is realized only by those who answer the call to help in response to their compassionate instinct. However, Grusha's decision to accept the burden of the child comes through her growing love for Michael, the helpless creature, as she watches him through the night; a love which finally becomes the bond between mother and son. The presence of the child provides her with an acute temptation to be a human being.

Too long she sat, too long she saw
The soft breathing, the little fists,
Till toward morning the temptation grew too strong
And she rose, and bent down and, sighing, took the child
And carried it off.

Even when Grusha realizes the sacrifice which her action demands, she conceives of that action in terms of its naturalness and its necessity:

Someone must help.
For the little tree needs water
The lamb loses its way when the shepherd is asleep
And its cry is unheard!

The *Lehrstuecke* mark Brecht's abandoning of natural images. It seems as if his attempt to control instinctive energy with a rational idealism made this discarding necessary. Nature, according to the imagery of the early work, was to Brecht the prime symbol of an irrational universe, chaotic and destructive. Nature became the symbol, as well, for those irrational energies which man felt within his own consciousness. In the words of Mr. Koerner, Brecht conceived of Nature as the source of "a diseased condition . . . something like a fever." [5] The meaningful identification of dramatic character with the natural elements which was consistent in the early plays, especially *Baal*, occurs only sporadically in the later plays (for example, in the association of Bloody Five's sexuality with the rain in *A Man's a Man*). The projection of the attitude of a character into the natural scene returns, richly and fully in *The Caucasian Chalk Circle*, after being anticipated in the language of *Puntila* and *The Good Woman of Setzuan*. However, in the naïve simplicity of the language of *The Caucasian Chalk Circle*, Nature is not the violent irrational force of the river in *Baal* nor the image of the planet earth hurled through space. Nature is not always benevolent and lovely in this fairy tale, but it does seem to exist as an expression or reflection of the sensitive emotions of its characters. Grusha teaches young Michael the beauty and benevolence of Nature; when the cold wind disturbs the boy, she comforts him with her poetic teaching:

> You mustn't fear the wind. He's just a poor thing too. He has to push the clouds along and he gets cold doing it. (*Snow starts falling*). And the snow is not so bad, either, Michael. It covers the little fir trees so they won't die in winter.

The wind is seen as a being like the small child, helpless and cold; and the snow itself performs a protective action which seems to find its natural source in the same motherly love which Grusha directs towards Michael. Nature, of course, is not pure benevolence. While it insures a season's protection in the home of Grusha's brother, it is also the source of her illness; and while Brecht's theatrical conception of the action marks the falling drops of the melting snow with the sound of the glockenspiel, that quickening musical rhythm announces the coming of spring, when Grusha must leave this protected place.

In Brecht's first play, the sexually devoured victims of Baal submit themselves to death in the black river, but in *The Caucasian Chalk Circle*, Grusha uses the icy stream for the baptism of the young Michael, committing him to life, not death. The insubstantiality of the memory of the absent lover is conceived in the reflected image of Simon in the stream. Whereas in *Baal* and the early poems of the *Hauspostille* the figure of the drowned girl, gradually decaying as she voyages the course of the river, keenly stated Brecht's acute awareness of mutability, this poetic image of the decreasing clarity of the lover's form reflected in memory contains no violent sense of decay. Rather it contains a pathetic response to the slowly fading dream of love and Grusha's attempt to keep her memory of it against the pervasive action of time:

> *As she sat by the stream to wash the linen*
> *She saw his image in the water*
> *And his face grew dimmer with the passing moons.*
> *As she raised herself to wring the linen*
> *She heard his voice from the murmuring maple*
> *And his voice grew fainter with the passing moons.*

When he returns to her, Simon stands beside the river, among the reeds. They confront each other in silence and their unspoken thoughts are voiced through the narrator. Simon describes the war in his imagination:

The battle began gray at dawn, grew bloody at noon
The first fell before me, the second behind, the third at my side . . .
My neck was set aflame, my hands froze in my gloves, my toes in my socks
I fed on aspen buds, I drank maple juice, I slept on stone, in water.

This scene—the anticipated meeting with Simon, returned from the war, and Grusha who has been forced by necessity to marry another in his absence—could easily be the most vivid demonstration of the aesthetic potential of the narrative technique of Brecht's epic theatre. Again, the two lovers speak in the third person, restraining their strong emotions in their own objective detachment. Ronald Gray writes:

> The lovers address each other at first in an exchange of proverbs which is both humorous and characteristic of their peasant origins. It is also, however, quite impersonal, a drawing on common tradition, and it is only by reflexion that the deep personal relationship between them is felt. In the climactic moment of the scene, in fact, neither speaks, and it is left to the narrator to reveal what each 'thought, but did not say.' Thus they confront each other in formal attitudes which are never realistically portrayed but are at the same time deeply moving, and it is by a similar estrangement that Brecht succeeds in making the outstanding human qualities of Grusha credible and acceptable.[6]

The mythical material with which Brecht is working in this play is a naïve and primitive tale, and as such it is certainly rich with archetypal associations. The presence of the recurrent image in German literature of the soldier's homecoming provides the danger of sentimentality. Yet here Brecht's keen theatrical sense and the poet's sensitive aesthetic have built a beautiful scene, removing the danger of sentimentality in the epic estrangement of the combination of restrained dialogue which is poetic in its structure of proverbs, narrative technique and pantomimic action. While the complex of techniques lacks verisimilitude, it focuses upon each character's essential response to the poignant situation with far greater clarity than the psychological diffusion of a more mimetic representation. Surely the tension between the unspoken thought and the present action is the real substance of the scene, and it is made possible in the division of word and action, or thought and action, in this epic narration. This tension reaches its most acute point as Grusha realizes that she has sacrificed Simon in her protection of the child, and she understands simultaneously that she could not have done otherwise. At this point she learns that Michael has been taken from her.

In *The Caucasian Chalk Circle*, the reality of social behavior is established by the corrupt princes. The play begins with the Governor's cruel denial of the beggars' and petitioners' cry for mercy. On the morning of Easter Sunday, the Christian celebration of the resurrection of a Savior whose death expiated the sins of mankind and earned the supreme mercy of Divine Grace, according to the Christian scheme,—the poor, the crippled, the unjustly accused are whipped back by the soldiers and dismissed by the Governor. Within the context of the play, Grusha's behavior is not essential but exceptional, and the realistic attitude of the other women defines her compassion as folly: "Grusha, you're a good soul, but you're not very bright and you know it. . . . Don't look at *him*. You are a fool—just the kind that always gets put upon." However, because her action is exceptional, it has a peculiar luster in the environment of the brutal soldiers, the vain and malicious Governor's wife, and the shrewish sister-in-law, Aniko. And while the happy resolution is the ethical consequence of both Grusha's goodness and Azdak's compassion, it is not typical.

In the dual structure of *The Caucasian Chalk Circle*, Grusha's dilemma is held in abeyance while the play proceeds to discuss Azdak, the judge who will solve the puzzling question. In the interesting structural division of the two stories, the lyrical celebration of Grusha's purity is balanced by the comic celebration of Azdak's misrule. Ronald Gray discusses Azdak as a reincarnation of Baal, in an extremely provocative comparison:

> Like Nature itself, he [Azdak] is ambiguous and amoral and requires the rebelliousness of humanity to bring out his qualities to the full. Then, however, when he meets with opposition, he reveals an unexpected generosity. . . . He is like Baal, it is true. But Baal was never opposed, lived his life in pure self-fulfilment, and died only to the tune of contempt from others. Azdak is Baal, and all that lies behind Baal, brought into relationship with human beings.[7]

Gray's conception of the integrity of Brecht's vision pro-
cedes from a perceptive understanding of the plays. However, while this critical identification of the two
heroes—who are divorced by twenty-six years and the
technical and philosophical development of the
playwright—has its justifications, the limitations of the
direct comparison can be misleading. Both characters
share a rich individuality, indulge in sensual satisfactions,
and maintain a strong appeal in their grotesque vitality;
and both seem to exist almost purely on the instinctive
level. However, the difference between Azdak and Baal is
stronger than Gray indicates. The primary focus of reality
in Brecht's first play is upon the existential consciousness
of the protagonist. All persons external to Baal seem to be
objects which exist primarily for his gratification. He
meets no opposition because nothing vital exists beyond
him; and his identification with the elements—the sky, the
rain, the river, and the trees—distributes his unique personality among the wide range of the natural scene. The
energy of Baal is the energy of the entire universe as
Brecht projects it, and Baal's world seems characterized in
Ekart's image: "The willows are like rotten stumps of
teeth in the black mouth of the sky." The sky is like a
great maw and so is Baal himself. Azdak is not simply
Baal "in relationship with human beings." Baal considers
other human beings merely as food for his consumption
and the whole world as excrement. Neither compassion
nor ethical commitment exist in the raw consciousness of
Baal which is sensitive only to hunger, gratification, and a
sense of surfeit. Azdak, too, is directed by an acute sensual
appetite, but his actions are also directed by compassion
and an ethical scheme, a deliberate program which is
certainly unorthodox, but which has an implicit, ethical
rationale.

Azdak's sense of justice is based upon a concept of
ethical relativity. He exercises the power he holds in terms
of each unique situation which he encounters, according
to the principle of a relative adaptation of ethics which
the Water-Seller asks for in *The Good Woman of Set-*

zuan. Wong asks the gods for a relaxation of the rules to suit the very bad times; he requests goodwill instead of love, good sportsmanship instead of morality, and instead of justice, outward propriety. Absolute goodness is held to be impossible in Setzuan's world of commercial exploitation. Shen Te asks:

> *Oh, why don't the gods do the buying and selling*
> *Injustice forbidding, starvation dispelling*
> *Give bread to each city and joy to each dwelling?*
> *Oh, why don't the gods do the buying and selling?*

In *The Good Woman of Setzuan* the presence of absolute goodness in humanity exists only in the apocalyptic fiction of "The Song of St. Nevercome's Day."

> *And the grass, oh, the grass will look down at the sky*
> *And the pebbles will roll up the stream*
> *And all men will be good without batting an eye*
> *They will make of our earth a dream*
> *On St. Nevercome's, Nevercome's, Nevercome's Day*
> *They will make of our earth a dream.*

In a sense, *The Caucasian Chalk Circle* is just such a dream. In the ethical scheme of the play, the existing social and political order is the irrational, consuming, and authoritarian commercial world of Setzuan enlarged to the political level of "The City of the Damned." The exploitation of the petty bourgeois of the earlier play is amplified into the corrupt exploitation of the workers by the war-mongering princes of Grusinia. In the truncated syntax of his imitation of the Grand Duke, Azdak describes the profiteering of the princes: "Did not send enough people. Embezzled funds. Sent sick horses. During attack, drinking in whore house." With this irrational standard as order, the misrule of Azdak's reign as judge becomes a kind of rational rule. On this level the grotesque behavior of Azdak—"The judge was always a rascal! Now the rascal shall be a judge!"—is the comic performance of the ritual of misrule, the comic repeal of authority. However, the sense of reason and compassion implicit in Azdak's justice makes his misrule a model of goodness unapproached by the previous plays. Even the selection of Azdak as judge, which is deliberately arbitrary and in the form of a jest, has its own logic. Certainly his evaluation of the nature of the Persian wars is more reasonable and valid in the mock trial than the fumbling performance of Bizergan Kazbeki, the nephew of The Fat Prince. Azdak's keen wit has pierced the hypocrisy of the corrupt magistrates. Playing the role of the Grand Duke, Azdak declares:

> War lost, but not for Princes. Princes have won *their* war. Got themselves paid 3,863,000 piasters for horses not delivered, 8,240,000 piasters for food supplies not produced. Are therefore victors. War lost only for Grusinia, which is not present in this court.

Consequently, there is a wry wisdom in the jest of establishing Azdak as judge of Grusinia. While Azdak's performance of justice is a kind of misrule, it is a misrule which sustains its own logic: not the objective application of formal principles, but as noted earlier, the subjective assessment of the relative situation in which only one principle is considered—that the rich should be fined, they can afford it, and the poor awarded. Consider Esslin's judgment that

> after [Brecht] had surrendered himself to what he regarded as a supremely rational creed, he depicted the rational side of his characters as an element of villainy in them—though one that was necessary for their survival in society. He, of course, always argued that after the victory of Communism this conflict between reason and instinct would disappear. But the fact remains that a practical approach to the problem of survival and success—such as the highly realistic tactics of Communism demanded—is consistently shown in a negative light in Brecht's later work.[8]

To the demand of survival, self-protection, Azdak is supremely irrational after he is established as judge. Before this "appointment," he demonstrates a Schweikian compliance in his declarations of guilt in the streets of Grusinia in order to be declared by others as innocent. However, as judge, his consistent work against the rich in a capitalistic society puts him in a precarious situation. His sensuous life is directed by his submission to emotion; however, his shrewd common sense directs a wise judgment of the cases presented to him, an instinctive perception of which decision will benefit those pleading before him and maintain an ironic gaiety in which the tattered undergarments of justice will be seen.

The first cases are given a greater confusion and assume a greater absurdity by being heard, according to Azdak's direction, two at a time. Consequently, two actions are juxtaposed with each other: a case of the patron of a doctor who sues the practitioner for professional negligence because he suffered a stroke when the doctor treated a patient with no charge and a case of blackmail. Here Azdak's sly wisdom chastizes the Doctor who, in the capitalistic society parodied, is unwise and foolish for not collecting his fee in advance, according to the usual mercenary practice of Grusinia:

> You are perfectly well aware that in money matters a good doctor is conscious of his responsibility? I once heard of a doctor who made a thousand piasters out of one sprained finger: he discovered it had something to do with blood circulation, which a less good doctor might have overlooked.

Azdak fines the invalid, the rich man in the case, one thousand piasters, but gives him the compensation of the treatment of his future second stroke free! The Blackmailer is condemned, but since his crime is against the rich his only fine is to share with the court one half of the proceeds of his profit, and he is advised to study medicine because of his keen financial sense. The folly of this first demonstration clarifies the humorous logic of Azdak's judicial decisions.

It should be noted that the first ritual procedure in Azdak's court is the acceptance of bribes. However, the bribery of Azdak has no influence on his decisions, merely upon his well-being; and, as he himself states, he likes to know the lawyer's fee "because I listen to you in quite a different way when I know you are good." In a context in which all judges take bribes, is not a judge who accepts a bribe and enjoys it without allowing it to influence his judgment infinitely more just?

With a pound you're on firm ground (no one is willing for
     a shilling)
     And the law is a cat in a sack.
But one whelp brings help to the many for a penny.
     The name of this rascal? Azdak.

Azdak is dirty, lecherous, cowardly; and yet, against the standard of behavior established by authorities who exploit and suppress the people, he is a hero; and his heroism derives from instinct. The invalid is fined, the doctor freed, the old woman's poverty comforted, the stableman's virtue recognized, and the daughter-in-law's voluptuousness enjoyed—all in a response which is instinctive. Like the altruism of The Young Comrade, that instinct is to act with compassion. Here Brecht's shifting response to a negative attitude toward rationality is demonstrated. In *Baal* and in *The Measures Taken,* the surrender to instinct results in chaos; and, when Azdak sings "The Song of Chaos," in celebration of "those terrible days" when his irrationality reigned, the order and beauty of that chaos is seen: the small man has joy and the authorities have complaints; the slaves are brought out into light; the hungry are fed; the rower becomes a shipowner. The song ends with the ironic plea:

> *Where are you, General, where are you?*
> *Please, please, please, restore order!*

The obligation which "The Song of Chaos" holds to certain sections of the Sermon on the Mount is obvious; and certain other references in the play, images and actions, suggest the parallels between Jesus and Azdak. Of course, the association of the dirty lecherous Azdak with the supreme symbol of pure compassion is a typical Brechtian irony. What it accomplishes, of course, is the reduction of an elevated figure of absolute compassion to the implementation of compassion on the most deprived human level. Azdak's compassion for humanity is defined by The Story Teller and Chorus in images suggesting the Biblical parallel:

Statute and rule he broke like a loaf to feed the folk.
On the wreck of the law he brought them to the shore,
Granted their shrill demands, took bribes from the empty hands
Of the simple and the poor.

The apex of Azdak's career as judge is his determination of Michael's true mother. In the trial, Natella Abashwili's greedy second lawyer reveals that "The revenue of her estates is blocked. She is cold-bloodedly told that it's tied to the heirs. She can't do anything without the child. She can't even pay her lawyers!" Of course the first lawyer is appalled at the stupidity of his assistant's revelation of this motive for Natella Abashwili's concern for her child. Yet his own description of the mother reveals something of her greed in its use of metaphor:

> High Court of Justice, she has conceived it in the holy ecstasies of love. She has carried it in her womb. She has fed it with her blood. She has borne it with pain . . . it has been observed that even the wild tigress, robbed of her young, roams restless through the mountains shrunk to a shadow.

The bestial nature of Abashwili is the primary truth of this passage. Against the elaborate rhetoric of the Abashwili lawyers, Brecht poses the simple truth of Grusha's claim and Simon's proverbs. Grusha says:

> I brought him up like the priest says 'according to my best knowledge and conscience.' I always found him something to eat. Most of the time he had a roof over his head. And I went to such trouble for him. I had expenses too. I didn't look out for my own comfort. I brought the child up to be friendly with everyone, and from the beginning taught him to work as well as he could. He's still a very little thing.

Although Grusha misunderstands Azdak's grotesque proceedings, he senses her virtue and her right to the child; and, like Solomon, he tests the claimants' love. In the test of the chalk circle, he clarifies which mother will allow her child to be hurt. Grusha, of course, refuses to pull the child out of the ring drawn on the ground, and proves the validity of her claim as she cries in despair, "I brought him up! Shall I tear him to pieces? I can't do it!"

Azdak's treatment of the rich, his helping of the poor and the exploited, is folly in the sense that it is the antithesis to the wise capitulation to authority. In these terms, his compassionate folly is irrational. At the end of "this brief golden age" of Azdak's justice—he quietly disappears, gradually lost in the dancers who celebrate the marriage of Grusha and Simon in a ritual *gamos*. Like a Messiah, Azdak has brought a very special era; and like a Biblical prophet, he experiences a kind of mystical departure, "after that evening Azdak disappeared and was not seen again." But for a while Azdak realized the dream anticipated in the vision of "St. Nevercome's Day."

Between *Baal* and *The Measures Taken*, Brecht began to associate human compassion with the self-consuming stream of life—destructive sexuality—which he had related to instinct in the first play. The Young Comrade who is willing to sacrifice his own identity, his own life, for the revolutionizing of the world provides a meaningful paradox. In this action, which is the logical consequence of his failure to suppress compassion, he performs the act of supreme compassion. The sacrifice of The Young Comrade is his act of consent and is generated from his own love of mankind:

> My heart beats for the revolution. The sight of injustice drove me into the ranks of the fighters. Man must help man. I am for freedom. I believe in humanity.

The suppresion of his own human feelings, necessary for the revolution, takes the form of the compassionate but suicidal act. Here the rational act and the compassionate act occur as one.

Compassion and destructive irrationality, in opposition to commercial efficiency and constructive rationality, form the schizoid personality of Shen Te–Shui Ta in *The Good Woman* of *Setzuan*. In this play, the heroine cannot exist with the rational identity of Shui Ta, but neither is she able to be happy without the goodness of Shen Te. At the conclusion of the play, the Gods do not exist as powers in a world in which love and compassion are absolute values; and the young girl, facing the responsibility of her unborn child, is told to compromise, to maintain a balance between compassion and reason. The accommodation of this conflict seems an impossible task and Shen Te projects the tension forward in her unanswered cry of "Help!" It is significant that the cruelty of Shui Ta has provided comfort and security for the parasites who attached themselves to Shen Te as a result of the efficient production of the tobacco factory. Here, as in *The Measures Taken*, the condition of ultimate altruism is approached by means which are immediately cruel:

> strength and wisdom are wonderful things. The strong and wise Mr. Shui Ta has transformed my son from a dissipated good-for-nothing into a model citizen. As you may have heard, Mr. Shui Ta opened a small tobacco factory near the cattle runs. It flourished.

Shui Ta is the imposition of reason upon the natural compassion of Shen Te; but this imposition does not provide a synthesis: rather it creates a tension which is not resolved in the drama. It would be too patent a judgment to say that Azdak in *The Caucasian Chalk Circle* provides a resolution of the tension projected forward at the conclusion of *The Good Woman*, because the combination of instinct and curious rationality in Azdak lacks the simple clarity that statement would imply.

The Caucasian Chalk Circle bears an interesting formal relationship with Brecht's didactic plays. In one sense, *The Measures Taken* is a supremely realistic play because its mimetic judgment assumes that the events which form the action of the play are real. Even the convention of theatrical performance is contained within this sense of realism since the act of impersonation is explained as a demonstration of actual events for The Control Chorus to judge and evaluate. While the assumption that the action upon the platform is a demonstration and not an attempt to create the illusion of present reality, the fact remains equally strong that the action holds a reality external to the stage. *The Caucasian Chalk Circle* is also a demonstration but it proceeds from a completely different mimetic judgment. As Gray notes, the prologue is an example of "soviet realism." [9] Here two collective farms are in dispute about a tract of land belonging to one of them, the goat-breeders. The members of the second collective farm want the land assigned to their use in order to fulfill their plan for an irrigation system necessary to their productivity. In order to justify the redistribution of land, a Story Teller, Arkadi Tscheidse, brings forward the performance of *The Caucasian Chalk Circle*. The fiction of the main drama is framed and justified within the naturalism of the prologue. However, unlike the demonstrations of *The Measures Taken*, the action of *The Caucasian Chalk Circle* does not assume a reality external to that which it imitates. Rather, the play exists as a parable, a fiction, which contains an implicit and obvious truth but which does not imitate a real action. Consequently, the degree of compassion and reason synthesized in Azdak is colored by the fact that a resolution of the conflict by the action of the "good-bad judge" is an obvious fiction. The narration of The Story Teller describes an age which approaches absolute perfection:

And after that evening Azdak disappeared and was not seen again.
The people of Grusinia did not forget him but long remembered
The period of his judging as a brief golden age
Almost an age of justice.

However, that "golden age" in which the compassionate moving of one human being toward another is rewarded in a survival which includes the gift of happiness is deliberately structured as an illusion. This romance, which contains the unique experience of an assertion fulfilled and rewarded, does not qualify the terms of Brecht's central drama, since it remains an illusion, a fiction, a dream.

In the Brechtian drama of the will, the values which are assigned to the individual consciousness and those which it encounters are varied and paradoxical. In one sense, the individual will which is undisciplined by any collective authority becomes a destructive agent, the helpless victim of the irrational energies of his own instincts. When he surrenders to these instinctive energies, he submits to a primitive, even bestial code of behavior in which one human being consumes another in order to survive. In the early plays, especially *In the Jungle of the Cities*, we see Brecht imposing this Darwinian metaphor of bestial survival upon the fact of man's exploitation of man in a civilized social structure. The paradox in Brecht's poetry develops in the very response to that exploitation. Those early works cry out against the presence of human suffering, against the exploitation of another human being; and yet, in those plays in which an ideal is posed in opposition to that exploitation, the ideal itself is given an ambiguous quality. In *The Measures Taken*, the ideal—the collective ethic of the Communist Party—is seen as a ruthless agency which destroys the individual. The movement of one human being toward another in love and compassion is seen as a surrender to instinct, a submission to those irrational energies which, if undisciplined, will destroy the will. The relationship of the individual to his own identity and to those other human beings which are his social environment remains, in Brecht, "in the loose of question." In the early plays, the human will is seen as the passive victim of its instinctive energies; in the mature plays, the will seems equally passive in its acceptance of that rational ethic which would demand that he submit, compromise, capitulate, scheme, and exploit his fellow human beings in order to survive. In these dramas, particularly *Mother Courage* and *Galileo*, Brecht intended to celebrate the human will which, in its commitment to some social good, would assert itself even if that assertion meant self-destruction. The assertion of the will in these plays becomes both a positive act and a negative act since it is both an assertion and a surrender to instinctive compassion. The assertion of the will affirms the value of human life—as Kattrin proves in her successful attempt to save the children of Halle—and at the same time denies its own life in an act which, in Brecht, is always suicidal. And yet, even though the "courage" of Anna Fierling actually represents an indifference to the value of human beings, an insensitivity, a callous growth created by years of capitulation which obscures her own compassion, her commitment to survival itself has a vitality and a value. Even though her commitment to survival is a capitulation and a scheming, it is also an election of life. In a sense, her very denial of instinct is the choice of life. In these terms, she has learned—as Kattrin never does—how to control the sudden onrush of instinctive compassion which is suicidal. However, the Brechtian dilemma exists in the fact that to choose life by denying instinct is to choose a life which is dessicated, mechanical, out of which all human value has been drained. That dessication is embodied in the image of the childless Mother Courage pulling her wagon after the soldiers, enduring only in her identity as the sutler-woman. And that dessication is clearer in an image of the wasted Galileo who suffers infinitely more than Anna Fierling because he can bear witness to the wide gap between the compassionate ideal of the birth of modern science and the selfish reality of his own capitulation. Like Fierling, Galileo elected life, and denied his instinctive movement toward a value outside his own will. However, his scientific contribution was generated in his total appetite for life; and he is unable to deny that very appetite which is the source of his scientific discoveries. Galileo realizes this; and in his immense guilt, his acutely suffering consciousness becomes the most fully developed vessel for the Brechtian dilemma of the will.

In *The Caucasian Chalk Circle*, Grusha makes that ambiguous Brechtian surrender to experience which is also an assertion of the will; she succumbs to the "terrible" temptation to save the child, but in the romance of this play, her assertion is not self-destructive. Here Brecht dramatizes an assertion of the will which, ultimately, realizes the identity of the human consciousness. In her act, Grusha becomes the mother of Michael, and, eventually, her goodness is rewarded with happiness. However, that curious prologue which has the quality of soviet realism certainly holds a more significant function than that of providing a polemic justification for the play. The prologue clarifies the unreality of the action which exists in reality as the aesthetic realization of the Story Teller and offers the delight and satisfaction of a lovely illusion,—an illusion in which the reward of compassion is celebrated as exceptional in a world in which compassion has only but a fragile and momentary life.

Notes

Introduction

1. Bertolt Brecht, *Seven Plays by Bertolt Brecht*, ed. Eric Bentley (New York, 1961).
2. Martin Esslin, *Brecht: The Man and His Work* (New York, 1961).
3. John Willett, *The Theatre of Bertolt Brecht: A Study from Eight Aspects* (London, 1959).
4. Bentley, "Introduction: Homage to B. B.," *Seven Plays*, p. xiv.
5. Esslin, p. 239.
6. Esslin, p. 253.
7. *Brecht on Theatre: The Development of an Aesthetic*, trans. and notes John Willett (London, 1964), p. 221.
8. Peter Demetz, "Introduction," *Brecht: A Collection of Critical Essays*, ed. Peter Demetz (Englewood Cliffs, 1962), p. 8.

1—Baal: The Celebration of Destructive Nature

1. Martin Esslin, *Brecht: The Man and His Work* (New York, 1961), p. 9.
2. Esslin, p. 9; Cf. John Willett, *The Theatre of Bertolt Brecht* (London, 1959), pp. 89–91.
3. Charles R. Lyons, "Brecht's *Im Dickicht der Staedte* and Albee's *The Zoo Story*: Two Projections of the Isolation of the Human Soul," *Drama Survey*, IV (Summer, 1965), 121–38.
4. Ralph Ley, "Brecht: Science and Futility," *Germanic Review*, XL (May, 1965), 208–9.
5. Claude F. A. Schaeffer, *The Cuneiform Texts of Ras Shamra-Ugarit* (London, 1939), p. 70.

6. Bertolt Brecht, "Baal," trans. Eric Bentley and Martin Esslin, *An Anthology of German Expressionist Drama: A Prelude to the Absurd*, ed. Walter H. Sokel (New York, 1963), p. 307. All further quotations from the play will be from this translation.

7. Willett, *The Theatre of Bertolt Brecht*, p. 90. Cf. Bernhard Blume, "Das entrunken Mädchen," *Germanisch-Romanische Monatschrift*, XXXV (1954), 108–19.

8. Sokel, "Introduction," *An Anthology of German Expressionist Drama*, p. xxix.

9. Sokel, p. xxviii.

10. Walter Weideli, *The Art of Bertolt Brecht*, trans. Daniel Russell (New York, 1963), p. 7.

11. Weideli, p. 6.

12. Brecht, *Tales from the Calendar*, prose trans. Yvonne Kapp, poetry trans. Michael Hamburger (London, 1961), p. 110.

13. Esslin, p. 278.

14. Hugo von Hofmannsthal, "Prologue to Brecht's *Baal*," trans. Alfred Schwarz, *Tulane Drama Review*, VI (Autumn, 1961), p. 219.

2—In the Jungle of the Cities:
The Isolation of the Human Soul

1. Eric Bentley, "Introduction: Homage to B. B.," *Seven Plays by Bertolt Brecht*, ed. Eric Bentley (New York, 1961), pp. xvi–xvii.

2. Martin Esslin, *Brecht: The Man and His Work* (New York, 1961), p. 280.

3. *An Anthology of German Expressionist Drama: A Prelude to the Absurd*, ed. Walter H. Sokel (New York, 1963).

4. Brecht, "In the Swamp," trans. Eric Bentley, *Seven Plays by Bertolt Brecht*, p. 3. All further quotations from the play will be from this translation.

5. This mythical scene is derived from several influences. Esslin notes: "Kipling was the main source of the exotic, mythical Anglo-Saxon world which forms the background to a great deal of Brecht's early writing. Other elements in it come from Swift and Gay, Upton Sinclair, Jack London, the Chicago stories of the Danish novelist J. V. Jensen (*The Wheel*), Dickens, innumerable crime stories, and gangster films." (*Brecht: The Man and His Work*, p. 109).

6. Martin Esslin, *The Theatre of the Absurd* (New York, 1961) p. xxi.

7. Bentley, "Introduction: Homage to B. B.," *Seven Plays by Bertolt Brecht*, p. xiv.

8. Northrop Frye, *Anatomy of Criticism* (Princeton, 1957), p. 212.

9. Bentley discusses Jensen's *The Wheel* as a source for the implicit homosexuality of the struggle for domination in a note to his translation of "In the Swamp," *Seven Plays by Bertolt Brecht*, p. 5. Bentley also notes the influence of the Rimbaud-Verlaine relationship as does Esslin in *Brecht: The Man and His Work*, pp. 108–9.

10. Brecht, *Selected Poems*, trans. H. R. Hays (New York, 1959), p. 47.

11. *Selected Poems*, p. 15.

12. *Selected Poems*, p. 51.

13. "Ballad of Cortez' Men," *Selected Poems*, pp. 33–35.

14. "Song of the Railroad Gang of Fort Donald," *Selected Poems*, p. 39.

15. *Selected Poems*, p. 15.

16. "Baal," *An Anthology of German Expressionist Drama*, p. 315.

17. *Selected Poems*, p. 63.

18. *Ibid.*

19. Esslin, p. 8.

20. *Selected Poems*, p. 57.

21. Esslin, p. 243.

3—A Man's a Man: Identity and the Collective

1. Eric Bentley, "Introduction: Homage to B. B.," *Seven Plays by Bertolt Brecht*, ed. Eric Bentley (New York, 1961), p. xvii.

2. Brecht, "A Man's a Man," trans. Eric Bentley, *Seven Plays*, p. 103. All further quotations from the play are taken from this translation.

3. Brecht, "A Radio Speech [27 March, 1927]," trans. John Willett, *Brecht on Theatre* (London, 1964), pp. 18–19.

4. Northrop Frye, *Anatomy of Criticism* (Princeton, 1957), pp. 169–70.

5. See chapter 1, note 13.

6. John Willett, *The Theatre of Bertolt Brecht*, p. 71.

7. Esslin, p. 284.

8. Ronald Gray, *Bertolt Brecht* (New York, 1961), pp. 44–45.

9. "Emphasis on Sport," *Brecht on Theatre*, p. 6.

10. "Emphasis on Sport," p. 8.

11. "Shouldn't We Abolish Aesthetics," *Brecht on Theatre*, p. 20.

12. "The Epic Theatre and its Difficulties," *Brecht on Theatre*, p. 23.

13. Kenneth Burke, *The Philosophy of Literary Form*, Rev. ed. (New York, 1957), p. 3.

14. Norman N. Greene, *Jean-Paul Sartre: The Existentialist Ethic* (Ann Arbor, 1963), p. 134.

15. Herbert Lindenberger, *Georg Büchner* (Carbondale, 1964), pp. 131–32.

16. Jean-Paul Sartre, *Being and Nothingness: An Essay on Phenomenological Ontology*, trans. Hazel E. Barnes (New York, 1956), p. 443.

4—The Measures Taken:
Instinctive Compassion and the Collective Ethic

1. Martin Esslin, *Brecht: the Man and His Work* (New York, 1961), p. 32.

2. Brecht, *Selected Poems*, trans. H. R. Hays (New York, 1959), p. 27.

3. Karl Marx, "Economic and Philosophical Manuscripts," *Karl Marx: Early Writings*, trans. T. B. Bottomore (C. A. Watts & Co. Ltd., London). Text published in Eric Fromm's, *Marx's Concept of Man* (New York, 1961), p. 168.

4. Charles R. Lyons, "Beckett's *Endgame*: An Anti Myth of Creation," *Modern Drama*, VII (Fall, 1964), p. 204.

5. Brecht, *Brecht on Theatre*, trans. John Willett (London, 1964), p. 8.

6. *Ibid.*, p. 30.

7. Esslin, p. 235.

8. H. R. Hays, "Introduction," *Selected Poems*, pp. 4–5.

9. Gray, p. 76.

10. Brecht, "The Measures Taken," trans. Eric Bentley, *The Modern Theatre*, vol. VI (Garden City, 1960). All further quotations from the play will be taken from this translation.

5—Mother Courage: Instinctive Compassion
and 'The Great Capitulation'

1. Bertolt Brecht, *Seven Plays by Bertolt Brecht*, ed. Eric Bentley (New York, 1961), p. 262. All further quotations from the play will be from this translation.
2. Franz Norbert Mennemeier, trans. J. F. Sammons "Mother Courage and Her Children," *Brecht*, ed. Peter Demetz (Englewood Cliffs, 1962), p. 145.
3. Mennemeier, p. 146.
4. Brecht, *Brecht on Theatre*, trans. John Willett (London, 1964), pp. 220–21.
5. *Brecht on Theatre*, p. 220.
6. *Brecht on Theatre*, p. 227.
7. *Brecht on Theatre*, p. 229.
8. *Brecht on Theatre*, p. 221.

6—The Life of Galileo:
The Focus of Ambiguity in the Villain Hero

1. Harold Hobson, *The Sunday Times* (June 19, 1960), cited in Ronald Gray, *Bertolt Brecht* (New York, 1961), p. 86.
2. Bertolt Brecht, "The Author's Notes on *The Life of Galileo*," *The Life of Galileo*, trans. Desmond Vesey (London, 1963), p. 14.
3. William Empson, *Seven Types of Ambiguity*, 3rd ed. (New York, 1955), p. 255.
4. I. A. Richards, *Principles of Literary Criticism* (New York, 1925), pp. 245–46.
5. James Smith cited in Empson, *Seven Types of Ambiguity*, p. xii.
6. "A Short Organum for the Theatre," *Brecht on Theatre*, trans. John Willett (London, 1964), p. 190.
7. "Alienation Effects in Chinese Acting," *Brecht on Theatre*, p. 94.
8. Martin Esslin, *Brecht: The Man and His Work* (New York, 1961), p. 229.
9. Esslin, p. 233.
10. Walter H. Sokel, "Brecht's Split Characters and His Sense of the Tragic," *Brecht: A Collection of Critical Essays*, ed. Peter Demetz (Englewood Cliffs, 1962), p. 127.

11. Allen Tate, *On the Limits of Poetry* (New York, 1948), p. 83.

12. Ernst Kris, *Psychoanalytic Explorations in Art* (New York, 1952), p. 256.

13. Gunter Rohrmoser, "Brecht's *Galileo*," trans. J. F. Sammons, *Brecht: A Collection of Critical Essays*, p. 117.

14. "The Author's Notes on *The Life of Galileo*," *The Life of Galileo*, p. 8.

15. This quotation and all further quotations from the text of the play are in the language of the Charles Laughton translation of the play included in *Seven Plays of Bertolt Brecht*, ed. Eric Bentley (New York, 1961).

16. "The Author's Notes on *The Life of Galileo*," *The Life of Galileo*, p. 14.

17. Rohrmoser, p. 117.

18. Rohrmoser, p. 120.

19. "A Short Organum for the Theatre," pp. 198–199.

20. "A Short Organum for the Theatre," p. 200.

7—*The Caucasian Chalk Circle*: The Dream of Goodness and Compassion Realized

1. Bertolt Brecht, *Selected Poems*, trans. H. R. Hays (New York, 1959), p. 25.

2. *Selected Poems*, p. 23.

3. Bertolt Brecht, "The Caucasian Chalk Circle," trans. Eric Bentley and Maja Apelman, *Seven Plays*, pp. 530–31. All further quotations from this play will be taken from this translation.

4. Martin Esslin, *Brecht: The Man and His Work* (New York, 1961), p. 251.

5. Brecht, *Tales from the Calendar*, trans. Yvonne Kapp (London, 1961), p. 110.

6. Gray, pp. 106–7.

7. Gray, p. 112.

8. Esslin, p. 253.

9. Gray, p. 103.

Index